#WARRIORWOMEN

Find your tribe
and live your best life

FIONA STUBBINGS

ISBN: 978-0-6484567-0-4

DEDICATION

To my boys, Jason, Harley and Beau, who represent the greatest
#WarriorWoman achievements of my life

To my tribes of #WarriorWomen who helped me birth this book
through support, love, inspiration and stories, they fill my cup
and I am the luckiest woman to know so many beautiful souls

To my darling Marlene

Thank you for your
beautiful friendship
& support
I hope you enjoy
the book

Fiona
X

CONTENTS

ACKNOWLEDGMENTS

Thank you to my friend and Editor in Chief, Janine Bilas. She has been the voice of reality and oh so gentle in her guidance on the content and format of this book. What a talent. What a support. One of the greatest #WarriorWomen I know. She inspires me to be better and do better.

Thank you also to my copy editor, Light Hurley who came in and tidied things up and cheered me on.

Thank you to my designer and friend Shelley Healy who designed the #WarriorWomen logo in the midst of her second pregnancy – another amazing #WarriorWoman with an abundance of talent and a heart of pure gold.

Thank you to my friends Julie, Kylene and Catherine who read my book and gave me so much useful and honest feedback – you don't get that from anyone else but your friends and I am forever grateful for their input.

Lastly, thank you to the women who participated in my research, who shared their thoughts, feelings, traumas and triumphs with me so that I could better understand women's experiences of life transitions. My research fuelled this book, my work and my passion to deliver services of value to #WarriorWomen everywhere so thank you my sisters.

ABOUT ME

Writing a book was never in my life plan. Not because I didn't think I could or didn't have an interest in writing. Quite the opposite - I love to write. Some of my earliest memories are of making up dramatic and comical stories and poems. I've also spent half my working life as a writer in policy work.

What led me to write this book was a series of events in my life that took me on a new path to a whole new career. Well, not completely new, I realise now that it's all very much related. This book is a result of my life transition, my a-ha moment, when I realized I needed to fulfil my purpose in this world and live my best life using the gifts I have been given.

I've spent the best part of the last twenty years working as a social worker. Trying to make a difference in the lives of children, young people, women, families and communities.

There were times when I knew I made an impact on people's lives for the better, but there were many times in my career when I had no idea what impact I was having, if I was having any at all. There were times I felt like I was stuck in a place where I had no impact on anything. I came to a point where I knew I had to do something else to help people, to help women like me who had experienced the things I'd experienced.

From a young age, I have always analysed why people do the things they do, what makes people tick. I've always been interested in helping people change unhelpful thoughts and behaviours. So when I found coaching I knew I was on the path for me. I knew that this transition was key to changing my life and key to fulfilling my dreams of helping other people to change their lives.

My dream is to help women and children to see that even if we can't control the things that happen to us as our lives change, we can control how we react to them and the thoughts we have.

If we sit back and think about all the thoughts we have, about our lives, about ourselves, about the situations we find ourselves in, and then we go and replace the unhelpful thoughts (those negative things we say to ourselves every day) with helpful, positive thoughts and beliefs, amazing things can and do happen. I know this to be true. I've experienced it. I am now on a different path in my life to the one I was on just four years ago.

I know I can follow my dreams. For no matter what happens to me, as long as I'm armed with the right strategies, beliefs and attitudes, and most importantly my sisters from other misters, my gang, my girl tribe, my #WarriorWomen – I will achieve my dreams, and I want to help you become the #WarriorWoman you were always meant to be. So you too can take your life to the next level.

ABOUT THIS BOOK

"The success of every woman should be the inspiration to another."

SERENA WILLIAMS

This book is for any woman who's been through a major life transition. Whether you've just had or are having children, changing careers or going through a mid-life transition. It's a book for all women. It's intended to show that we're not alone. That we can build a community of #WarriorWomen together, wherever we are.

A NOTE ON THE #WARRIORWOMEN SYMBOL

The symbol on the front cover is the #WarriorWomen symbol of unity. The symbol of a triangle represents the strength of women. The lines interconnect and lift, showing that it is not one single woman alone, but rather the tribe of women supporting each other who have the greatest strength.

Having tools and strategies at hand to help you navigate through the changes in life more positively and with a focus on the future is my hope for you. The messages within this book will help you to realise that you can have whatever it is you want if you truly believe you can. Yes, I know how cliché that sounds, but there's so much truth behind it.

I want you to take your life to the next level of happy. To aim for and start to plan for bigger, brighter and more fulfilling lives filled with success, joy, love and the support of your #WarriorWomen tribe.

This book may also be helpful for coaches or people with an interest in supporting women through life transitions like pregnancy, parenthood, career change, or navigating the work and family balancing act.

The literature I have read on women's life transitions is either very health or clinical focused. I was looking for something that addressed the needs of women, whilst also proposing strategies to move them through the transition and so this book attempts to do just that.

Throughout, I'll offer coaching tips and strategies and NLP (Neuro Linguistic Programming) techniques for navigating your life forward in different areas. I hope they help you to see ways to turn the crappy parts of major life transitions upside down, so their power over you and your future is gone! These strategies are for taking you to the next level, where you can live your best life.

Check out the Appendix for an explanation of NLP.

1

INTRODUCTION

" *A strong woman stands up for herself. A stronger woman stands up for everybody else"*

ANON

I've spent the best part of a year surveying and talking to #Warrior-Women about their major life transitions as part of my research for this book. With their permission I'll be sharing some of their thoughts throughout the book.

My research has shown me that not only are all women #Warrior-Women because they face challenges head on and fight hard to come out the other side, but also that there's a sisterhood code that makes us all want to support, uplift and help each other. I'm constantly amazed by the number of women out there helping other women to make their lives amazing.

What set me off on this journey and fascinated me about this topic were the changes in my own life... and the realisation that I actually didn't know when I was going through a major life transition myself.

After I entered the world of coaching, I thought about my experience of becoming a mother and how it had changed me in so many ways. The thing is, I didn't actually acknowledge it at the time. I knew other women must have been through similar experiences and felt the same way I did but, like me, kept on going, thinking we'd get through the changes somehow. I now call it 'muddling through life'.

Little did I know that with a bit of help focusing and addressing my fears and beliefs, I could've come through that transition with so much more clarity, purpose and focus on my future, as well as my children's futures – it's not as selfish as you might think!

Major life transitions

After establishing my coaching business, Mind Design Coaching, I wondered if it'd benefit women to become more aware of what life transitions are, when they happen or are likely to happen, and how they can get through those times of major change with more focus, direction and positive intention.

Life transitions can be anything from taking on a new job, moving house, to becoming a parent or getting divorced. They are represented by feelings of being stuck in a place or moment, reaching a crossroads and not knowing which direction to take or wanting to change your life but not knowing what/how to change. They can also simply be a major change in your life.

Mind Design Coaching helps women to identify, navigate and triumph through these life transitions to live their best life imaginable. Because

I can't meet all of you amazing #WarriorWomen face-to-face, I've written this book to help those of you I can't work with personally.

We all have a story to tell. A story that can and will help other women experiencing similar things. Sharing our stories is what make women's lives better. By sharing your own story with other women you are helping and supporting them during their time of change and transition, and this can be a gift of immeasurable value.

This book is about honoring #WarriorWomen all over the world — women who are navigating major life changes and all that comes with it. This book is for all #WarriorWomen and anyone who wants to know or work with them.

May we stand together in battle and celebration always.

If you only read a chapter or the whole book, I hope that you close it with a new found energy to get on with making your goals, hopes and dreams a reality. Get on with it beautiful, strong #WarriorWomen and...

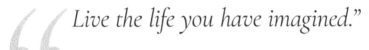

Live the life you have imagined."

HENRY DAVID THEREAUX

If you need more information about coaching or life transitions, please visit my website, minddesigncoach.com.

2

#WARRIORWOMEN

> *A woman is like a teabag. You can't tell how strong she is until you put her in hot water."*

ELEANOR ROOSEVELT

SO WHAT IS A #WARRIORWOMAN?

Every woman is a #WarriorWoman.
Every woman I know.
YOU...
And every woman you know.

We've fought the battles. Some we've won, some we haven't.

Some #WarriorWomen wear their scars on the inside, where few can see them and even fewer get to know them. Some wear them on the outside, like badges of honour and strength.

Whatever we've gone through, we're all #WarriorWomen. We all have our own stories of joy and love, pain and sorrow. We're together on this adventure we call life, all navigating as best we can with the resources we have.

#WarriorWomen aren't born warriors. No one I've met was born a warrior. We become warriors by how we choose to deal with the many challenges and adventures we encounter.

SUPPORT THROUGH MAJOR LIFE TRANSITIONS

Elizabeth Kubler-Ross made some great insights into humanity. You'd probably recognise her work on grief and loss. She postulated the Five Stages of Grief and Loss; denial, anger, bargaining, depression and acceptance. She defines #WarriorWomen inadvertently and beautifully:

'The most beautiful people we have known are those who have known defeat, known suffering, known struggle, known loss, and have found their way out of the depths. These persons have an appreciation, a sensitivity, and an understanding of life that fills them with compassion, gentleness, and a deep loving concern. Beautiful people do not just happen.'[1]

I love this. It speaks to so many of the qualities of #WarriorWomen. We become stronger and more empathetic through life's battles.

From here on in, #WarriorWomen will be known for their strength and courage in the face of change and, most importantly, for standing beside other #WarriorWomen to lift them up.

---

[1]   Elizabeth Kubler-Ross, 1969, On Death and Dying

YOUR TASKS

Throughout this book I will be setting you tasks. Some of them might not be relevant to you now, but at some other point in your life they will be. The tasks are for you to sit with, reflect on and then act. One of the key components of coaching is that once you have defined and decided upon your goals, nothing will happen until you take action.

So, before you go any further with this book, I would love for you to reflect on your Warrior past. Think back to a time when you went through a major change in your life.

Take your time. Get a visual picture of the event (one that stands out to you). Feel the feelings you had. See the images. Hear the sounds from that time in your life.

Now write down your response to some of the things below:

What were you feeling?

_____

_____

_____

What did you do? How did you respond to the change?

_____

_____

What was good about the experience?

_____

_____

_____

What did you find out about yourself that was positive/ surprising?

_____

_____

_____

What was missing from your life that you wanted?

_____

_____

_____

What would you do differently now? (if anything)

_____

_____

_____

What resources did you use? Think about internal resources such as will power or determination, and then external resources such as friends, family, community

_____

_____

_____

What resources did you need that you didn't have? (both internal and external)

_____

_____

_____

This exercise arms you with a list for the future that defines some (or many) of your:

- Strengths
- Needs
- Resources
- Approach

It's helpful to reflect on difficult experiences, what you needed more or less of at the time and also what you can do to prepare for future change.

Even though my style of coaching is future focused, I think every experience in our lives teaches us something about ourselves. It's important to know your barriers or blocks. Then you can change them and take your life to the next level.

As you read through the relevant chapters, keep in mind your warrior past. Reflect on your strengths and how you would do things differently in the future with the strategies and tools in this book.

Now I want you to write down here a list of strengths you have recognized in yourself.

_____

_____

_____

These are the things that helped you through the change or event. They are the things that you became as a result of the change and the things that drove you to get through it. With this list, pick out some key strengths, the ones that make you feel the strongest and most positive about yourself. Now go grab some post it notes or paper and write them down on separate pieces and place them randomly around the house so that you are reminded every day of your gifts and your #WarriorWoman strength!

To change your thoughts and beliefs about yourself you need to re-program your brain. Writing and repetitively reading positive things about yourself helps to set down new neural pathways in your brain and quite literally changes your mind!

3

YOUR TRIBE

#WARRIORWOMEN ARE AN AMAZING TRIBE

Whenever life gets tough or exciting (or even when it's a bit same old), I turn to my tribes – yes you can and should have more than one. I couldn't live without my girlfriends. They are essential to my life's happiness.

Whether you have a girl tribe, a squad, a girl-gang, whether it's your mum, sister, neighbours or relatives, whatever you want to call them, whoever they are, you need them.

The traditional definition of a tribe doesn't quite fit my life and maybe that is the case for yours too. As I mentioned before, I have more than one tribe. I have girlfriends from all over the world and across different parts of Australia and even Sydney. Some of them know each other and some have never met, so its ok to have more than one tribe especially when different people meet different needs in you. Your tribes could have one or two people in them or twenty people. So when I talk about my tribe or tribes, I'm really just talking about the women in my life who provide support, love and friendship at any given time.

There is something so special about the unconditional love and support our sisters provide us. There is something empowering about having women in your life who know everything about you and still love you!

If you don't have a tribe or tribes, now's the time to find yours. (If you can't find a tribe or don't know where to start, contact me and join my Facebook/WarriorWomen Wellness Group.)

The driving force behind this book is my passion for the power of women. Women who stand together and uplift each other.

EVALUATING YOUR TRIBE

A couple of years ago I had what some might describe as a mid-life crisis. I like to call it the 'depression I had to have'. It was a real low point in my life and I found out who was there to support me and who wasn't.

The experience of what I now believe was a mental breakdown allowed me to take stock of my female relationships. Who was going to help me get through this, without judgment, without people fearing they would 'catch it' (I'm pretty sure some people think mental illness is catching) and without gossiping about me behind my back? I had to take stock and take control over the people I shared my life with so I could live the extraordinary life I wanted.

I did a whole lot of soul searching, as you do when you face a crisis! I realised we women need our girl tribes. We need friends and family who'll lift us up when we're having trouble doing it ourselves. We need friends and family who don't stand and judge. We need friends and family who get right down on the floor with us when we fall and say, 'I'm here, let me help you get up, do you need wine?'

OUT WITH THE NEGATIVES...

Throughout my life I've suffered from depression. It comes in waves. I suffered ante- and post-natal depression with both my children and I know how easy it is to go to dark places in your mind.

The thing that got me through those times (apart from my husband and boys) was my girlfriends, especially the ones who'd been through it themselves.

Taking stock of my friendships meant I sifted through the good, the bad and the downright awful (thankfully, there weren't too many of those). I made a promise to myself to nurture the good, which when you have depression is not as it easy as it sounds. You need to make an effort to go out, to make plans, to get dressed when you don't much feel like facing the world.

However, it turns out, spending time with your girls is one of the best antidotes to depression.

The next step was to bench the bad, either not spending time trying to maintain the friendship or spending less time with Debbie Downers.

Finally I had to fire the downright awful friendships in my life. These tend to be people who have nothing positive to say, who talk about other people with venom and who just don't make you a better person by being with them. I used to want to heal these wounded birds, and I still do, but in coaching I learned that my future and my life is the only thing I can control.

The process liberated and empowered me. When you ditch the unhelpful relationships in your life, you're left with way more time to nurture the good.

Maybe you have been feeling this way yourself and don't know how to handle the friendships or relationships that bring you down. Stay with me. I have some tips at the end of this chapter.

IN WITH THE POSITIVES

So, as I said before, I set about trying to keep the beautiful and inspiring women in my life, and I let them know how much they're appreciated. It's hard running businesses, studying, working and managing family life. However, it's the most rewarding thing in the world to spend a few hours with our tribe, just being ourselves.

Now that I've got a better perspective on the women in my life, I want to support other women to empower each other, cheer each other on and fix each other's crowns – to succeed, to live their best lives and to love life!

What I realised is if we have people behind us cheering us on, we have more capacity to succeed. Why? Because when other people believe in us, we begin to believe in ourselves, and when we believe in ourselves, that's when the magic happens.

YOUR TRIBE

Not one single person meets all of your needs all of the time. A tribe is an opportunity to have a bunch of girlfriends who meet our different needs.

There's a school of thought that suggests we become the five or six people we surround ourselves with in our life. That's pretty enlightening when you think about it. So who do you want to be? Who needs to be in your life?

When you are thinking about who you have or need in your tribe, I suggest you think about the following types of friends you could or should have in your life (or make up your own if you prefer). These are just ideas. You can probably come up with one or two more. Here are some examples of the types of women you need in your tribe...

1. A #WarriorWoman Tribal Chief

Everyone needs someone who has been there before. Whether you take advice from others or not, having a wiser more experienced friend in your life is always helpful when it comes to making big decisions. She's the one you trust to know what she's talking about!

She's probably a few years older. She's had a few more experiences than you. She'll still be fun but she will know just what you're going through and what you might need. She will guide you lovingly. Needless to say, she's a keeper.

2. A #WarriorWoman Trail Blazer

This friend is connected. She knows people and can hook you up with everything from a great osteopath to the latest technology. She always has new and fabulous ideas or solutions to everyday problems. She sings your praises to her every contact – you need her in your life because she just oozes positivity and success!

3. A #WarriorWoman Fan Girl

This friend cheers you on, tells you to go big or go home. They are your biggest fan. They're positive about everything you do and they want to see you succeed. They're probably very successful themselves They see your worth and your talent and they support your every move with as much excitement as you, maybe even more! From singing your praises to liking your every social media post, they go out of their way to share your gifts with the world.

4. A #WarriorWoman Empath

This friend has totally got your back. You can cry on her shoulder and she will always listen and comfort without judgement or offering unsolicited advice. She knows you just need an ear and a great big hug. She is your comfort, she is your security when things get crazy. She is pure love. She won't let you go through anything alone.

5. A #WarriorWoman Truth Doctor

This is the friend you go to for the absolute honest, straight down the line, no holds barred, truth about whatever it is you want, need or are about to do. It's the brutal honesty you need when you might be all tangled up in emotions and can't see straight. She won't sugar coat. Every #WarriorWoman needs a Truth Doctor who isn't afraid to tell you how it is. If you are open to criticism, open to honest feedback and can take the truth from someone you love, this person will be invaluable to your life and your future.

6. A #WarriorWoman Fun Fitness Friend

This is the friend you exercise with. She wants to do fitness events with you and go on adventures. She will run, walk, cycle, swim, lift weights with you and make you accountable to your physical health. She will have you back when you don't feel like running at 8:00pm at night. She will tell you to "go straight home, do not stop at the bottle shop, do not think about take away, get your gear on and get to the gym, I'll see you there". This girlfriend is priceless in terms of your health and wellbeing. Exercise is key to maintaining good mental health as well as physical health. You can't do without her.

If you think you might need more of any of these women in your tribe and less of the ones you have right now, then you need to do the friend stocktake here and now.

There will always be hurt feelings in a friendship stocktake. Being sensitive to other feelings is important when you choose to make any kind of significant change in your own life, especially one that has an impact on another person's life. But, being afraid of hurting someone's feelings is not a good enough reason to keep people around who keep you down. You can do this, I believe in you.

THE FRIENDSHIP STOCKTAKE

If after reading this chapter you feel like you should do a stocktake on your friendships, there are a number of things you can do.

Step 1 – Sit for a minute. Think about your current friendships. Who are the women in your life? Who do you see often and who not so often? Write a list on a separate piece of paper (in case you want to loan them this book ☺).

Start by asking yourself (write it down below): 'How do these people make me feel?' This exercise will help you to attach your fabulous tribe members to all those good feelings.

_____

_____

_____

On the flip side you may have friends (or family) who make you feel bad about yourself, or depressed, but you keep them in your life because you feel sorry for them or guilty or responsible etc.

This is where you need to ask yourself: 'What do they bring to my life, what is their purpose in my life?'

_____

_____

Do I need or want them to continue to be a part of my life?

_____

_____

What are my beliefs around this person and our relationship? What do you believe this person brings to your life?

_____

_____

It's important to do a check-in on your beliefs. The answer to many of our blockages or inability to change stem directly from our core beliefs around an issue.

Only you can decide if these women are truly part of your tribe.

When you work out who you really want in your tribe, ask yourself: 'What do I need to do to maintain and grow the relationship?'

_____

_____

Step 2 - Creating your list in Step 1 will help you to determine who's missing from your list. This is key to stepping up your networks and bringing into your life women who will help you to become the person you want to be, the person you're meant to be.

Ask yourself 'Who else do I want in my tribe that isn't already in it, and why?' Think about people you admire, respect, look up to, want to learn from.

_____

_____

Now ask yourself: 'How can I go about meeting women like that to build my tribe?' Here you need to step outside your comfort zone, go out and network! You might need to go to conferences or join facebook groups or reach out personally to these women.

_____

_____

CALLING IN THE NEW - INITIATING THE NEW MEMBERS OF YOUR TRIBE

We don't always meet like-minded people by chance. Sometimes you need to throw yourself at people and see if they catch you. You can't lose what you don't have. If people don't respond to you, maybe they're not meant for your tribe, or maybe you need to convince them that they need you too!

One brilliant resource we now have is social media. For all its faults there are so many benefits. Meeting people through networks you belong to can lead you to those people you most want to be like and have in your life.

You can search for pages on Facebook by subject matter, profession, hobbies or geographic locations. The possibilities for joining new groups is endless – remember to ask yourself if these groups add to your tribe.

When I was in the party styling business, I found a divine woman doing these amazing chocolate piñata cakes. They look like cakes but they are made of chocolate and you smash them like a piñata that is, of course, full of lollies (you have to get these for your children they are crazy fun. Find the lovely Kylene at Smashcake. com.au). I immediately wanted them at my parties so I contacted her. Eight years later she is one of my most treasured friends. Thank you Facebook. I'm living proof you can meet and make genuine connections with like-minded people (who also might love chocolate) via the internet. BTW we often laugh about how our relationship started on the internet.

TIES THAT BIND

Sometimes changing your circle can also be a major life transition. If you've had the same friends for forever (say, since high school or longer) and have never done an assessment of how they make you feel, it may well be a big turning point in your life.

You may feel a bit stuck here, like you're at a crossroads. That's okay. Change like this is hard and its ok to take your time with it if you don't want to rip the band-aid right off.

Believing we should come first in our own life is often something we women find hard!

But I can assure you, once you decide to make the change for yourself and choose to put yourself first, the friends who love you and want what is best for you will stick by you. What kind of friend wouldn't want you to be happy?

The best way to tackle a major change like this is to follow the steps above. Remember that you need to firstly believe you are worthy of more from your friends, and secondly that you need to be around people who **value** you, **respect** you and bring **happiness** and **joy** to your life. If you aspire to be an entrepreneur, then you need to surround yourself with people who inspire you, develop you and make you better (you'll find literally hundreds of them on Facebook, Instagram, Snapchat, LinkedIn etc).

Breaking ties with people who've probably leant on you to feel better about themselves, but not offered the same in return, can be hard. Take your time, explain your reasons (if you have to) and let the friendship die a slow, natural death if that helps you to feel less guilty.

There's a quote that has stuck with me for many years that I reflect on when things change in my friendships (it's very relevant to romantic relationships, too). People come into our lives *'for a reason, a season and a lifetime'*.

Embrace the reason, enjoy the season and never take for granted those you have for a lifetime.

Now that you have done the friend stocktake you need to take action. Write down the first few things you will do this week to get moving on re-organising your tribe.

1. What is the first step you will take to move you towards creating or building your totally awesome and uplifting girl tribe?

_____

_____

_____

2. When will you do it? (be exact with date and time if necessary – it has to be this week)

_____

_____

_____

3. Who will you tell you are doing it? (for accountability – partners are good for this kind of thing)

_____

_____

Put it in your diary and make the commitment to start on your path to building your tribe of #WarriorWomen.

You can post to either of my Facebook pages *#WarriorWomen Wellness Group* or *Mind Design Coaching* where my tribes can support you along the way.

4

MAJOR LIFE TRANSITIONS

'Change is the only constant.'

(HERACLITUS, 6TH C BCE)

This book is about taking major life transitions and making the best of the **opportunities** they present.

My biggest lessons in life have come from understanding that what we think, feel and believe alters how we experience the world. We have the power to change our thoughts and feelings. Even the significance of our memories. We have the power to think and believe what we want, to seek out what we want and in doing so we can move forward and leave those bad bits behind us.

Don't get me wrong. I don't think there's any way of reconciling the death of a child or loved one or taking that pain away. I don't wish to minimise that pain or suggest it doesn't exist. I don't disregard the very real physical and emotional pain of heart break and divorce. Nor the struggles of becoming a parent and deciding how best to manage work and family life. Sometimes pain is necessary. We need to sit with it a while to learn their lessons, to grow and to become the people we are meant to be.

CHANGE AS OPPORTUNITY

I believe we can change our own world by changing how we think about it.

Take a moment to process that. What thoughts and beliefs about yourself or the world are consuming you? Or bringing you down? Or making you feel bad about yourself?

Take this opportunity to write them down here

_____

_____

_____

_____

_____

Now, imagine not having them. Imagine you have positive, future-focused, exciting thoughts and feelings instead.

Try replacing the things you wrote above with the opposite positive thoughts, feelings and beliefs.

What does it feel like to flip unhelpful thoughts on their head (pun intended)?

_____

_____

_____

_____

You may just feel a little lighter and brighter.

Now I want you to choose one or two of the positive key words you wrote down above. Choose the words that resonate with you the most. These are your **power words**. They will give you strength and positivity when you need them the most. These are your words. They have the power to change your life.

Write the words down and put them in your wallet, on your wardrobe door and bedroom mirror – wherever you will see them often.

MAKE THE CHANGE

We all know change can seem hard, awful and scary. However, if you believe it to be an opportunity for personal growth, to make lasting and positive changes to your life that will take you to a more empowered level in your life, then they will never again seem hard, awful or scary. You might actually get excited about the prospects of change!

In this book I may mention the crappy things that happen to us women, because I want to highlight what makes us #WarriorWomen, and it's about being real, showing you that you're not alone and that you are absolutely not going crazy (alone).

Yes. Your experience is uniquely yours, but someone somewhere in the world can always relate to it. This is what connects us as #WarriorWomen. It's what makes us special to each other. It's what brings us together in a way that we can share the joy and the pain. It's what I love about the 'sisterhood'.

More importantly, it's about taking those real life moments and choosing to see the opportunities in them.

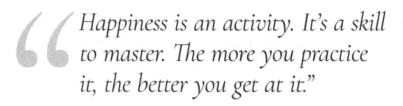

> *Happiness is an activity. It's a skill to master. The more you practice it, the better you get at it."*

RICHARD BANDLER

Whatever goals you set yourself or whatever life transitions you're going through, the ultimate goal is to come out the other side happy, right?

To be successful in achieving happiness, particularly through major life transitions, you'll need to change the way you think and the language you use to talk to yourself and others.

Start with being kinder, to yourself and others. This is the most important factor in changing negative beliefs and feelings you may have about yourself.

One of my favourite Richard Bandler[2] quotes is:

---

[2]   Note: Richard Bandler is best known as the co-creator (with John Grinder) of Neuro-linguistic programming (NLP), a methodology to understand and change human behaviour-patterns (see the Appendix for a deeper explanation). His approach is a no-nonsense, common sense approach to changing the way you think about yourself. Once you practice it a bit you will soon find it's easy.

"Feelings and emotions are not things we have, they are things we do. We create these feelings through what we do inside our head."

A lot of what you'll read in this book will be about making changes to the things you do *inside your head*.

You have a choice to think and feel whatever you want in any situation and when you are going through life changes its easy to get caught up in unhelpful thinking.

Choose to speak kindly to yourself. Seek out the happier more positive thoughts and you will see how it changes everything in your life.

A WORD ON BELIEFS ABOUT YOURSELF

As you have probably guessed, I'm a huge fan of NLP and neuro-science. Much of the work in NLP is about changing beliefs and unhelpful ways of thinking about yourself and your life (see Appendix for more on NLP).

If you truly believe you can achieve what you want, you'll find a way to achieve it. You see there's a feedback loop where what you think and believe determines how you act, which then determines what results you get, which then determines your beliefs.

According to Richard Bandler, happy, successful people have a lot of useful beliefs about themselves, their goals and the resources to achieve them.

Reality is not as fixed as you think. You can change your reality. You can change your beliefs.

CHANGE YOUR MIND – DESIGN YOUR LIFE!

Just before you move on, here are a few questions to help you identify your level of happiness and the language you use inside your head.

You might want to find a quiet space and get comfortable with a cup of tea (or a glass of wine):

Now, I want you to think back to the time when you last felt really, truly, blissfully happy. Try to get a visual picture in your head – spend a few minutes on this.

Where were you?

_____

_____

What can you see?

_____

_____

What can you hear? (if anything)

_____

_____

What are you saying to yourself in this moment?

_____

_____

What are the defining features of this moment that made you happy?

_____

_____

_____

Now come back to the present moment and answer this:

How can I feel that way more often?

_____

_____

_____

What do I have to do or change?

_____

_____

What resources do I need?

_____

_____

Now you need to write down 3 things that you will do this week to help you get back to your happy place and find your bliss:

_____

_____

_____

Write these three things down on a piece of paper and post it somewhere you will see it often.

Work on these things daily.

Practice visualizing yourself in your happy place regularly and check back in on how you are doing with achieving your weekly goals.

SECTION 1: MUMOLOGY

THE PSYCHOLOGY AND PATHOLOGY THAT IS BEING A MUMMA

MUMOLOGY

5 BECOMING A MUMMA

'Making the decision to have a child – it is momentous. It is to decide forever to have your heart go walking around outside your body.'

ELIZABETH STONE

So many things in life bring about major life change but nothing quite like becoming a parent.

This is where we women get to experience one of life's most amazing adventures; the good, the bad, the ugly and the amazing!

When planning for children (or not), we tend to focus on the little bundle of joy who'll come into our world, turn it upside down and bring with it huge amounts of joy, love... and sleep deprivation.

We all know there'll be pain, so much pain! I remember my neighbour saying to me in passing one day as I approached my due date, "It's gonna hurt", and me thinking, "Really? No woman on the planet's going to deny that pushing a watermelon out of a grape-size hole won't be painful."

What we don't think about and what we don't talk about, is how our **identity** and sense of self will never be the same again.

Becoming a parent changes you forever.

Who we are is divided into two distinct life stages - **BC (Before Child) and AC (After Child).** Once we become mothers, we become something else, and that something else is different for all of us. The one thing that's the same is that we're changed by this event.

For some women this is a welcome and exciting change. Dreams come true. The ache to be a mother is satisfied, the need to nurture, care for and unconditionally love a tiny, helpless, perfectly designed little human is fulfilled.

For other women (like me), the change is a mix of highs and lows, positives and negatives, and we don't find it immediately the empowering, life-affirming experience we thought it was going to be. This might have been your experience too.

I have put some exercises in the following chapters to help you address some of the identity challenges we face before, during and after having a baby. These tools will help you to coach yourself through the uncertainties of parenthood when you are just not sure what is happening.

MUMOLOGY

6 THE NEW YOU

LET'S START AT THE BEGINNING - YOUR NEW PREGNANT IDENTITY

Our identity starts to change from the moment we start trying for a baby and then when we find out we are pregnant. We start to focus on things we never had second thoughts about before, like whether we can eat runny eggs or not.

There's so much to learn!

During pregnancy we begin to realise that our body is not our own anymore. There is a precious tiny human living within us, sucking the life out of us (more often than not) and draining us of our energy. We are no longer the sole focus of our lives. We have this little person growing inside of us that has top priority and we have to give up wine and soft cheese for a bloody long time!

For very active people, pregnancy can be quite confronting if we are feeling unable to exercise. I was a six-times-a-week gym junkie. I could barely get out of bed from nausea that stayed with me all day and all night like a hangover that just kept giving (but without the fun from the night before).

Needless to say, I couldn't identify with this sick and tired human I'd become. I didn't know who I was if I couldn't train every day and get my 'fix' – I had no idea how to solve the problem. There were no answers. I couldn't think straight. I just wanted to go to bed, every day, usually five minutes after I got out of bed.

I'm pretty sure I was stuck in pregnancy hell and I know I'm not the first woman to feel that! This may have been your experience too? Or worse (bless your soul you are a true #WarriorWomen, don't ever forget that)!

What I needed was direction. Some small steps I could take to meet new fitness and health goals. I needed to find strategies to reconcile my former self with this new self and focus on what I COULD do. Because when big changes happen, a lot of us tend to focus on what is lost, what we can't do anymore, what we don't have anymore and how bad that makes us feel (which by the way doesn't help us get out of the funk).

So if that's where you are at and what you are feeling, here's some coaching advice. To live our best life we need to focus on what we HAVE, what we CAN do, what is GOOD and how we can make it BETTER – we need to think about the solutions rather than the problem to keep ourselves focused on the positive.

This is how we change our neural pathways inside our brain (more NLP). This can and will lead to changing our brain chemistry. There is a lot of neuroscience behind this. Trust me.

If you are feeling a bit stuck, like you have lost part of yourself or something from your life right now, here is an exercise to help you re-focus and bring back some positive energy and re-focus your thoughts.

The best place to start is with **gratitude.** Being grateful has a way of making us happier, healthier, more likeable, more optimistic and less materialistic and self-centred.

This exercise is great for anyone feeling stuck in a moment of change – so you don't have to be pregnant to do this one.

What are all the things I am grateful for right now?

_____

_____

_____

What am I looking forward to most about this next phase in my life, for example being a mum?

_____

_____

_____

What is one thing I can do right now to help myself feel better? (For example, take time out to rest every day, meditate, have a cup of tea and read a book, take a nap etc.)

_____

_____

_____

How can I make sure I do these things regularly? (Be accountable to yourself and your self-care. Block out time in your diary, get your partner/parent/friend to remind you, get others to do household chores while you rest – yes it is possible!)

_____

_____

_____

Try to focus on the solutions. Get your tribe and your family members involved wherever you can – they can take your washing for you and do it, they can clean your house while you nap, they can do you grocery shopping.

It's time to initiate the tribe for this next phase of your life. Get them working for you now before the baby comes so they are well trained for when the baby is here!

MUMOLOGY

7 PREGNANCY PLANS PLANS PLANS

During pregnancy, we're susceptible to doubts and fears about the future, about what's in our control and how we can take back control.

Some of us might be worried about work. How to get up every day to get there. How to maintain a sense of professionalism when all we want to do is lie down on the floor and nap for four hours (Okay, that might've been just me).

Most of us feel the need to plan for our 'next life' where there's a child and we'll have to juggle work and family life.

In actual fact, most of our pregnancy revolves around planning. What furniture to buy. What childcare centre do we enrol our child in. Which one is the cleanest. What will we do if we don't have child care in time to go back to paid work – Shit, can that happen? How will we budget when we are off paid work? What's a budget and can I live without new shoes for a year? How will we manage a child and a career at the same time – My boss wants me back asap? What responsibilities will the baby daddy have? – He has enough trouble looking after himself. What kind of parents will we be? – For the love of god, nothing like our own. How many books should we read – Is ten enough? What kind of pram will we need? If it's not $3000 will it still work properly? What kind of nappies should we use – Geez there's more than one kind?

And the questions go on!

So many things to plan for and already we are becoming something that we were not **B**efore **C**hild.

It's at this time that women need to actively prioritise and plan for how they will leave their job, what to expect, and how they will manage both the practical and emotional changes a baby brings. Really you have no idea what is coming your way – so plan for the expected and the rest is a lovely surprise!

WHAT ABOUT WORK?

Maternity coaching offers employers an opportunity to support their valued staff in the transition to parenthood whilst helping them to also maintain contact with the work place and ensuring strategies are in place for both the employer and employee ater the birth.

So if you have access to coaching, take it. If you don't, here are some serious questions you can consider in your planning.

COACHING QUESTIONS DURING PREGNANCY

Below are some questions you can ask yourself during pregnancy to help you set down work and family priorities and goals for after the baby arrives. Bear in mind, though, some of these may change after baby arrives, so it's a good idea to review them again at regular intervals like at three, six and twelve months after baby arrives.

What is my vision for my life short term (for the first twelve months after baby) and long term (at five and ten years) for both career & family?

Short term

_____

_____

_____

Long term

_____

_____

_____

What are my career goals?

_____

_____

_____

What do I need and want from my employer when I return
to paid work?

_____

_____

What do I WANT my life to look like when I return to paid work? (this might be different to what you THINK your life will look like)

_____

_____

_____

Again, these can and most likely will change after the baby arrives so keep checking in on these goals when you have the brain power again.

Keep track of your goals, write them down in a journal and review them on a monthly basis.

I offer maternity coaching to women and organisations where I coach women before they go off on maternity leave, during mat leave, just before returning to work and just after returning to work. This ensures both the employee and employer have clear goals and plans set out. These can be revised as things change during this massive life transition. It also helps organisations to support their valued staff – because happy staff stay, right?

MUMOLOGY

8 WHEN BABY/ANGEL FACE ARRIVES

When the baby arrives, most women either have the shock of their lives and some form of post-birth post-traumatic stress (I mean that in all sincerity) or they've had a lovely birthing experience that went seamlessly and according to plan. It might have been something in between. Whatever it was for you, it was the start of a new and amazing chapter in your life.

I had two very different birthing experiences: the first was incredibly frightening and traumatic, and left some mental scars that hung around for years; and the second wasn't so traumatic, but was very clinical.

On the bright side, given I have an oddly positioned pelvis and RH negative blood type, if I'd become pregnant 200 years ago, I'd probably not have children today or I'd have died in child birth with my baby.

Neither of my experiences were fun, but that didn't change the love I felt for my baby boys, who became the centre of my world instantly. I feel incredibly lucky to have safely birthed two beautiful, healthy, spirited precious boys! Awwww!

No one woman's experience in birthing their child is the same, and we, as #WarriorWomen, carry the experience with us forever, regardless of whether it was traumatic or not.

What helps following birth is to be encircled by our tribe, fellow #WarriorWomen, who can let us know we're not alone.

What you might need to do at this time is reach out to your tribe. Many of us are not sure whether to interrupt this special bonding time with your baby or not so you need to let your tribe know what you prefer and need.

If you are not feeling the 'specialness', now is the time to call the girls over – get them to bring food, wine (if you are able to drink it yet), and share your experiences with them. Your friends will jump at the chance to be a part of the special time and also have a squeeze of the baby. So if you need them, let them know.

There are also a lot of things that don't help at this time which friends and family really need to be aware of.

You know who they are: the mother/mother-in law/friend talking about how "Our Sonny never did that" or "My birth was so much worse" or "you should be grateful for a healthy baby" (My response: yes, indeed, I should, but I don't need you to tell me that after having 3.5 kilos quite literally ripped out of my vagina, thank you). Or my personal favourite: the smug mother with "I did that three... four... five times" (NOT HELPING!).

My point is that being smug isn't helpful. Support, love, listening, nurturing and empathy is. So shut up with the advice, bring the food and love and listening ears – leave your preconceptions at the door.

As #WarriorWomen who've birthed our own children (or even if you didn't go through the birthing process to bring your babes into the world), we share this magical experience. So we need to band together and support each other during these times. We have the benefit of knowing what's coming for our fellow #WarriorWomen and it's not always fun!

If you are a new mumma, or about to become one, it is worth writing down the people you know who will support and nurture you after baby arrives.

Who can I call if I need help with?

- Cooking food for the family

_____

- Getting the shopping done

_____

- Having a shower (as opposed to a bird bath)

_____

- Going for a walk/getting out of the house with company

_____

It's a great idea to talk to your friends and family about how they might be able to help you with these and other things. Things like the washing/vacuuming/cleaning. If you have a Caesarean birth you won't be able to move around easily for a few weeks at best so you will need people on hand. Partners are good but sometimes they are also a bit freaked out and unable to think clearly.

There's nothing wrong with setting expectations for your support people. If it means they get to come around and see the baby more often then you know they will be super excited to help out.

WHAT WILL I DO IF I FIND I'M NOT COPING WITH MOTHERHOOD?

Every mother at some point in the early stages (and all other stages) of parenthood feel a bit wobbly. You will have these moments and you probably won't see them coming.

Talk to those in your tribe who are mums already. Talk about how they handled their wobbly moments where they felt like they weren't coping. The sisterhood will save you, I promise, but you have to be honest. We come from a society where we have to be 'seen' to be coping all of the time or we feel like a failure.

If you are not coping well, having a bad day, week or month, you need to reach out for support. Your tribe is where you will get it. If things are especially bad and you are thinking dark thoughts, thoughts about harming yourself or your baby, then you need to seek urgent medical attention.

The numbers to call are both below and in other chapters of this book. (If you are not in Australia, please look up the numbers on the internet for post-natal depression or ask your ante-natal support person for the contact details). Keep them handy for when baby arrives:

Lifeline   131 114

PANDA - Post & Antenatal Depression Association panda.org.au

The Gidget Foundation –

www. gidgetfoundation.org.au 1300 851 758

Beyond Blue beyondblue.com.au

The Black Dog Institute   blackdoginstitute.com.au

Parentline   132 289

Lifeline suicide helpline   1300 651 251

What you need to keep in mind is that these feelings are not failure. These are very real and common experiences. If you are armed with a plan, you will be better equipped to cope if it happens to you.

Talk to your family and ask someone to be your contact if this sort of thing happens to you, or any kind of wobbles where you feel you can't cope.

MUMOLOGY

9 THE HOMECOMING SHOCK

So, baby arrives into the world. We feel all those wonderful feelings of unconditional love, euphoria, contentment, joy and being absolutely overwhelmed! We may also feel fear, terror, anxiety. What's next?

We take the baby home. We have no idea what to do with said baby. Then here comes the reality....... the person we once were is gone forever. Here's this new person in their place – the mumma, the mummy, the mother, the parent, the person forever responsible for another human life. Wow! As far as life transitions go, this one is big!

It's now that we start to realise we had no idea what was about to happen to us. We think about other women, our friends who've gone through this before us, and think:

'What the hell? Why didn't they tell me?'

'Why is this so hard?'

'Why is this little person so demanding (...so beautiful, but sooooo demanding)?'

'How am I going to survive on this little sleep?'

We need so much support, love and nurturing ourselves at this time, but it seems we have to do all that for someone else! If we have a great partner, then we get some respite. We're able to work as a team. If we don't, we can very quickly become isolated and disconnected.

When I had my first child and we went to the clinic for our 'classes', one piece of advice a nurse shared that stuck with me (and I unashamedly share with every pregnant person I come across) was that new mothers need four hours alone time per week to maintain base level mental health. That's a base level, not flourishing or thriving mental health.

My first thought was 'wow, that's not much. Don't we get more than that?', but then I set about organising those four hours.

At the time, I was lucky enough to have my sister (my chosen support person and life saver) come over to help out on Friday afternoons, so when my baby was six weeks old, I went back to the gym. However, there was that minor detail that I was breastfeeding three hourly. I could get about two-and-a-half hours alone time at the most in those early days and that was like project managing the opening ceremony to the Olympics – or at least it felt that way!

It was challenging to meet those four hours. The second time around, I didn't get four hours 'alone time' until he was eighteen months old. That kid wasn't having me leave him for anything. I'm still waiting for him to cut the umbilical cord and it's looking like I may have to wait until he's at least eighteen years old.

So my point is it's easy to see how we #WarriorWomen can begin to lose our minds if we don't look after ourselves and set in place some strategies for self-care.

If you're a new mumma here are some things I want you to think about:

How am I looking after myself at the moment?

_____

_____

_____

If your answer is 'I'm not' then how can I look after myself better – what can I (or other people) do for me?

_____

_____

_____

Don't stop there, what else can you do?

_____

_____

Who can help me get some alone time? (If you don't have family or close friends nearby, think about neighbours, a local nanny service – Facebook is great for finding resources quickly.

Ask around and try a few different options.)

_____

_____

What resources do I, or the helpers, need?

_____

_____

When will I make it happen?

_____

_____

Now lock it in with your support person. Put it in your diary, and theirs, on a weekly basis. If they can't do it every week, find some other people and get a roster happening or get someone to set up a roster for you.

This might feel awkward. You might feel guilty or even ashamed for being 'needy', but I can tell you right now you are none of those things. You will be forever grateful for setting this up early and setting down the expectation that you need to look after yourself too. Again, remember, they get baby cuddles.

I know this is hard. It was hard for me. I actually didn't want to leave my baby, either of them. I thought I was going to do damage to them by 'abandoning' them, but it's not true. They will be okay. You won't be okay, if you don't look after yourself properly.

Here are some other helpful numbers that might come in handy in the early hours of the morning or any other time you feel like you need some advice.

Tresillian – live advice 5pm-11pm Monday to Friday online at tresillian.org.au or 1300 2 PARENT 7am-11pm Monday to Sunday

Karitane – 1300 227 464 karitane.com.au

We need so much support, love and nurturing ourselves at this time, but it seems we have to do all that for someone else!"

MUMOLOGY

10 FIRST TIME MUMS

Motherhood – all love begins and ends there."

ROBERT BROWNING

COACHING FOR THE FIRST-TIME PARENT

Those women who take to motherhood like a duck to water, feeling like all their dreams have come true and never wanting to do anything else with their lives but make babies, probably don't need coaching at this major life stage.

For the rest of us, coaching can be a powerful intervention at a time of massive change.

To reflect on the past and look to the future allows women who are feeling wobbly and uncertain to maintain a sense of purpose, direction and identity.

Mums of all kinds are a special kind of #WarriorWomen because they have gone into battle. They have fought an intensely painful and physical fight to bring new life into this world.

Who said we have to be selfless about it all, though? Now, more than at any other time in our lives, is the time for us to invest in ourselves, in our mental health and in our future selves.

I've spoken about the changes and the support we need in those early days. This section is about taking it to the next level and helping new mummas to maintain a sense of self and a strong identity post baby.

COACHING NEW MUMMAS

New parents need help with navigating this new role and identity of being a mother. Many of us have very little knowledge about how to care for a child, we have only just established good practices in caring for ourselves (mostly), so this new role can be scary.

Fear is a common reaction to becoming a new parent. Fear of stuffing up, fear of losing our mind, fear of never feeling normal again, fear of dropping the baby!

Coaching for new parents needs to respond to the ridiculous amount of changes that are happening and focus on the strengths of new mothers, their abilities and resources available. Ensure they get through this time feeling positive and successful. That's what coaching can do.

If you are a new mumma and have been diagnosed with post-natal depression and you're receiving professional help, having a coach or trying out these tips and tools can be a huge help in creating a positive mental attitude. They can help you change negative thought patterns and help you to look forward to an amazing future. This does not replace any kind of psychotherapeutic interventions or medications, but can be a great complimentary resource.

The following exercise can help you to find your strengths and the resources available to you.

COACHING ACTIVITIES AND QUESTIONS
FOR THE NEW PARENT

What's good in my life (baby-related and non-baby-related)
right now?

_____

_____

_____

What's going well?

_____

_____

_____

What can be better?

_____

_____

How can I make it better?

_____

_____

_____

What resources are available to me to have my needs met?

_____

_____

_____

Who can help me/support me? (repeating again here just as a reminder)

_____

_____

Who can look after the baby so I can get some baby-free time? (If you don't answer anything else in this book – make sure you know the person or people who will do this for you)

_____

_____

NOTE: To be clear, coaching does not replace mental health services for women experiencing post-natal depression. If you or someone you know is experiencing depression or anxiety they/you can't get out of or find release from, please seek help (the numbers are throughout this book and at the end of the next chapter).

MUMOLOGY

11 ANTE-NATAL, POST-NATAL DEPRESSION

" *This is an illness that takes away a woman's ability to access joy, right at the time she needs it most.*"

DR. KATHERINE WISNER

'm no expert on post-natal depression, but I've had it twice. I've also had ante-natal depression twice. I've been treated for depression for both.

Firstly, any kind of depression needs to be treated by a professional, whether it be your GP, a psychologist or psychiatrist.

Some elements of depression can be improved through NLP, and I work on my own depression symptoms using some of these strategies. I'm a firm believer that you can change your thoughts and, therefore, change the way you feel. I'm also a firm believer in psychological/psychiatric interventions and medication, should they be necessary.

PMDD - PMS ON STEROIDS

My own experiences of depression have come and gone. Hormonal imbalances are what I believe to be the biggest cause of my depression over the years, and I've suffered from a condition called Pre-Menstrual Disphoric Disorder (PMDD). PMDD is basically PMS (pre-menstrual syndrome) on steroids!

It hasn't been a well-known or publicly addressed condition and it's not an easy one to diagnose. One of my best friends also suffers from it, and I thank the universe for bringing her into my life because having someone who knows exactly what it's like has been sanity saving. (Again, there's nothing that can beat the support of fellow #WarriorWomen.)

PMDD has the same characteristics as PMS, but the emotional and physical symptoms are more debilitating for example severe/clinical depression, rage are some of the symptoms. It's caused a lot of problems in my relationships in the past, but I'm now able to manage it so much better. One day, I'll set up a support group for PMDD sufferers, so if you experience it, contact me. I want to hear from you.

Having experienced PMDD and PMS, and also depression prior to pregnancy, there was a greater chance of me experiencing ante-natal and post-natal depression.

MY ANTE-NATAL DEPRESSION

My experience of ante-natal depression was not fun. I struggled with pregnancy and not being able to do the things I wanted to do. I felt unwell (severe and constant nausea) all the way through both my pregnancies.

The ante-natal depression I experienced in my second pregnancy was worse than the first. I imagined not being around anymore (yes, dying) a lot. I fantasised about it, because I wanted to be well and feel myself again but couldn't see an end to my feelings. I should've sought help, but based on my previous pregnancy, I knew I'd feel better as soon as the baby arrived so I 'toughed it out'. I don't recommend this to anyone.

However, after the second baby was born, the relief from feeling unwell was short lived. I started to become depressed again quite soon after he was born. He didn't sleep much and wanted to be held a lot. I found myself sitting on the lounge in the same spot every day for days on end, just holding this baby who wouldn't go down. Eight months into his life, I was thinking about walking into the ocean and not coming back out (Yes, dying. Again!). I desperately needed and wanted to find relief from the sleep deprivation and feelings of being so inadequate.

I thought I was doing something wrong. I wasn't. I found out two years later that my baby had sleep apnoea so he was never going to sleep properly without medical intervention.

Thankfully, I reached out for help and got it (thank the universe for an Australian health system that's resourced and responsive when it matters most in a woman's life). Once I filled in that mental health questionnaire at the clinic, the troops got to work and got me some help. I also went back on anti-depressant medication. Just having people around me, letting me know I was supported, was exactly what I needed. I could've had it sooner if I'd reached out before it got so bad. Again, I don't recommend you 'tough it out' for ANY amount of time. Be honest with yourself.

LONELY DAYS

Sadly, I also felt more alone with the second baby than with the first. This was because I didn't go to the clinic regularly or to a mothers' group. Because it was my second baby, everyone assumed I knew what I was doing, and for the most part, I did. But the baby was different from the first, the experience was different. I felt even more pressure to 'know' what to do, when I had absolutely no idea!

Isolation is one of the biggest issues for new mothers and we are not very good at talking about it. If you're feeling alone, exhausted and not sure how to get through each day, please reach out to your child health nurse, GP/Doctor, the hospital you gave birth in, a shrink of any kind, a friend, whoever you can find.

Also get on to Facebook and search for support groups/pages. Get on to Pinky Mackay (her Facebook page saved my sanity and made me feel like nothing was abnormal and I was doing the best job possible). Reading comments from other mothers in similar situations can also help to make you feel 'normal' and not so alone. You can also get tips and ideas you may not have tried.

Just because you need it now, doesn't mean you'll need it forever! I think this is an important point – you're not going crazy. You're tired, exhausted, spent and you need a break from it all.

If my story has triggered you in any way, please contact lifeline, PANDA or Beyond Blue on the numbers below. Please, never wait for things to 'get better' on their own.

Lifeline   131 114

PANDA - Post & Antenatal Depression Association www.panda. org.au

Beyond Blue www.beyondbue.com.au

The Black Dog Institute   www.blackdoginstitute.com.au

Parentline   132 289

Lifeline suicide helpline   1300 651 251

MUMOLOGY

12 WHO AM I?

In my conversations with women and through my research, I've found that the feelings commonly experienced by new mothers are something like:

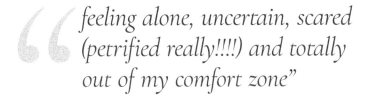

feeling alone, uncertain, scared (petrified really!!!!) and totally out of my comfort zone"

New mothers can often feel disconnected from the 'real world', living day-to-day like its Groundhog Day, with little connection to the outside world. These feelings of isolation and disconnection can turn a highly effective, intelligent, super-functional woman into a confused, emotional mess (I'm pretty sure it's not just me).

If you have just had a baby you might be asking yourself questions like:

'Who am I?'

'Who's this person who hasn't showered in three days?'

'Why does my partner get to shower, go to work all day and be around grown-ups, drink hot tea/coffee, eat an entire meal in one sitting and be able to string their thoughts together without interruption?'

Then there are these questions:

'How long does this last?'

'Why can't I pull myself together enough to get me and my child out the front door?'

'Why is there so much crap on day-time television? What market are they actually targeting, because it can't possibly be women with half a brain?

While most of us love our babies beyond words, we're also thinking:

'What the heck?' and *'How did this happen to me? How can a reasonably smart, strong, ambitious woman be reduced to a pyjama-wearing, rambling, bi-polar crazy lady?'* (Or, was that just me again?)

The thing is, we're not quite prepared for the identity crisis, especially those of us who went from one extreme to another. From the ambitious, high functioning career focussed woman, to the pyjama wearing sloth. We have always known who we are and what we wanted out of life.... or at least who we **were**.

We are in a fog of raging hormones. A storm of sleep deprivation, sore, cracked, bleeding nipples, pain sitting down, pain standing up, pain moving any body part connected to our pelvic region...

These things are generally how we experience our world for the first six to eight weeks after our baby arrives, and it's unsettling to say the least.

SO, WHAT ACTUALLY HAPPENS TO US?

Here are a few of the most common issues women experience after bringing baby home:

- We're tired from lack of sleep (understatement).
- We don't much like what's happened to our body (new floppy bits in random places).
- We doubt our abilities to parent.
- We have crazy mood swings that come from nowhere.
- We can't fit into our clothes and feel like we'll live in maternity wear for the rest of eternity.
- We stress about work and our role at home and what role we actually now have in life!

I'm sure you have felt at least one, if not all of these things since having your child/children, I know I did.

On the upside, it's not all bad! Becoming a parent also brings with it love (so much love), a sense of fulfilment, a time of growth and development, the discovery of new skills and abilities that we find in our nurturing and mothering (particularly the things we learn to do with one hand!).

Personally, I found my creative side. After having my first child I found my left brain seemed to kick in and I wanted to make stuff.

THE SECOND IDENTITY CRISIS

I've talked about the changes in our identity and life when we first fall pregnant. Let's return to that. Once the baby arrives, we have a second identity crisis, or challenge.

In the early days we are at home a lot, getting used to our new family member and life. Sometimes life can become mundane and boring. Not that we don't love it but, let's be honest, babies eat, sleep (sometimes) and poop. There's not much more to it.

This is now our new role in life. Our full-time role for however long we choose or need to be off paid work. We're now tasked with keeping another human alive at all costs. Usually, this costs our sense of identity, our mental health, and our ability to function cognitively and physically.

The real shock comes to us when we realise we're now this other - AC - person.

We're a mother, so we go to mothers' groups (if you're lucky to find like-minded mums you want to hang out with). Our conversations turn to feeding, the colour of baby poo, the sleep we haven't had, the sleep our baby hasn't had, the sleep our partner HAS had and how that 'other' person - the person we were BC - is gone. How we don't know if or when we're ever going to see her again.

Getting used to this new identity (not to mention a new family member) takes time. You have to wrestle with priorities and needs and your sense of self. Just when you think you know who you are and where you're headed in life, this baby throws you a curve ball and you have to re-evaluate all over again.

If you're feeling a bit confused about who you are now, you might want to reflect on your sense of identity and think about where you are at and whether it is where you want to be in your life. It always helps to think about the future and what you want from it.

Try this little exercise below:

1. What are your thoughts and feelings about being a parent right now at this time in your life?

    _____

    _____

    _____

2. Now spend a few minutes thinking about your future and your future self, say one year from now. What you will be doing and who do you want to be? Get a visual picture of your future in your head. Feel the feelings, hear the sounds, see the pictures.

3. What kind of parent do you want to be?

    _____

    _____

    _____

4. Who do you want to be in 12 months time? What will you be doing with your life?

_____

_____

_____

5. I know it might be a stretch to think about this now but give it a go if you can - Who do you want to be in 5 years time? What will you be doing with your life?

_____

_____

_____

_____

What resources do you need to achieve this life?

_____

_____

_____

_____

Where will you get the things you need?

_____

_____

Now write a list of all the things you can do right now. The things you can do to start working on achieving that life you see yourself having in five years' time. Keep the list somewhere where you can see it often. Keep those things in mind, because even though you are all caught up in the world of a tiny baby right now, when you repeatedly visualise your goals, you will bring those things into your life.

_____

_____

_____

_____

_____

_____

_____

MUMOLOGY

13 LOOKING AFTER THE MUMMA

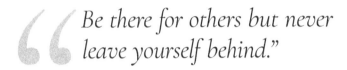 *Be there for others but never leave yourself behind."*

DODINSKY

Every stage of being a mumma can bring with it challenges. Keep in mind though that challenges are opportunities for growth.

Being a parent means life is constantly changing. Setting ourselves up with resources and skills to manage these changes as they happen in our lives is the best tool we can give ourselves. Just when you think 'I've got this', something changes. Life throws you a curve ball. If you have the tools and resources by your side, you will navigate the next phase with so much more confidence and ease. Being a mumma is the toughest and most amazing job you will ever do – so you need to be the best version of yourself!

TAKING SOME TIME OUT

Along with keeping future focused and setting goals we also have to look after our own well-being.

I know I have said this a lot already but, asking for help so we can look after ourselves by taking time out is key. Call the people you are closest to and maybe set up a roster like I suggested in Chapter 9.

Self-care is the single most important thing a mother can do for herself, her family and her children.

Below is a goal setting activity for the here and now. If you can follow something like this now, you are way more likely to manage the day to day business of being a mumma more easily.

SELF-CARE TIPS FOR THE MUMMA

The best way to take care of yourself is to plan it into your day.

1. Write down your daily and weekly plan. Get a wall planner if it helps. On the planner, block out time for yourself each day (even if it is ten minutes a day, block it out). You could also do it in one long block somewhere in the week instead.

2. Plan some form of exercise, like a walk. (It doesn't have to be long or bootcamp-style training, just get your body moving.)

3. Plan self-care time, like a massage, a coffee with a friend or a pedicure (these don't have to be baby-free in the first couple of months - most babies sleep and can sleep through a pedicure. If you need to breast feed, remember you're among women and

they couldn't care less if you get your boobs out and feed your baby). Do one self-care thing a week (not including exercise).

4. Make sure you're getting out of the house almost every day and you'll start to feel like a participating member of society again.

Take care of yo'self, Mumma, and the rest will fall into place.

MUMOLOGY

14 BACK TO WORK – IT TAKES A VILLAGE

RETURNING TO WORK

Going back to work after baby is a big deal for most women. It's not easy thinking about leaving our babies with other people. Sometimes, many times, these strangers don't know our baby's needs. I actually remember mine as a gut wrenching experience that came with so much guilt. It isn't that I didn't want to return to work and be a working mum, it's just that I didn't want to leave my babies. For some mums they feel guilt because they want to return to work. These conflicts we women feel about balancing work life and family life are real throughout our children's lives, and they can often feel impossible to resolve. Remember it takes time to find the right balance, support and resources.

The guilt is just a part of being a parent – it's not a helpful emotion, in fact it's a useless emotion. We need to flip those thoughts and feelings on their head because they don't serve us at all.

If you are feeling a huge amount of guilt, feel paralysed and unable to make decisions because of it, go back to chapter three. Do the exercise on changing thoughts again. Right now you need to be focused on getting your work life back and you need to be having positive, future focused, helpful thoughts.

EMPLOYER SUPPORT FOR RETURN TO WORK

Because most women go back to work after having their babies in Australia, for a long time now I've considered it the role of employers to support their female staff throughout the pregnancy journey. Not because I want to shirk mine or my family's responsibility, but because I believe it's the responsibility of the community we live and work in to support each other. It really does take a village or tribe to raise a child.

We women continue to strive for equality in the workplace, yet need the flexibility to maintain work/life balance so that our children and families can function effectively.

In a previous nation-wide inquiry, the Australian Human Rights Commission found that one in two Australian women experience discrimination during pregnancy and/or their return to work. Further to this, 84% of mothers report negative impacts on their mental health, physical health, career/job opportunities, financial stability and families.[3] These are shocking numbers. They show how far we have to go before the women who are raising the next generation get the full support of the community.

When an employer has a valuable employee, why would they not want to do all they can to support that person to navigate life transitions effectively and efficiently and enable them to transition in a way that benefits everyone?

---

[3] http://www.humanrights.gov.au/news/stories/pregnancy-report-reveals-personal-and-financial-cost-discrimination

COACHING SUPPORT FOR RETURN-TO-WORK

As you can tell, I am a huge advocate for employer support for parents. The benefits of providing coaching supports to women in the workplace are tri-fold:

1. Women who feel supported by their employers want to remain with that employer post-child birth and probably return to work sooner – this leads to better retention of good employees, less turnover and less money spent on the training and induction of new employees.

2. Women who feel valued by their employers are more motivated to perform well, which leads to better productivity.

3. Women who are able to plan for their return to work in a way that meets theirs and their employers' needs are, in turn, more flexible when the business requires them to be. This creates a win-win situation for both employee and employer.

These aren't small things. They're big challenges. I know there are organisations doing this already, but there's a long way to go before it becomes common Human Resources practice. Many organisations don't yet realise the benefits of supporting their fabulous female staff.

MATERNITY COACHING – WHAT IS THAT?

I touched on this a little earlier - Maternity coaching is a holistic support that focuses on both the personal and professional lives of women. Personally, women are coming to terms with the losses and gains of their new role, as well as work/life balance. Maternity coaching is valuable at all stages of the major life transition such as:

- during pregnancy, to plan and prepare for maternity leave,
- whilst they are on leave to plan and prepare for their new life and plans for their return to work and,
- when women do return to work, to set future career goals within the organisation and support the transition process.

All these processes support a committed, motivated, positive and future focussed female workforce and for organisations to be family friendly, flexible and future focussed, they need to have a maternity coaching program (and yes I do offer these in my coaching practice).

My point is, now that we've left the 1950s behind us, it is not just our friends, family and community services that form the village we need to raise good humans. Employers and organisations have a responsibility to support their #WarriorWomen staff more holistically as well.

TASK

If you are planning your return to work right now, here are some questions to think about that will help you and your employer prepare. It might also be useful to suggest your employer provide you with some maternity coaching:

What resources do I need to go back to work? E.g. Child care, flexible work start and/or finish time, reduced hours/days, work from home etc.

_____

_____

_____

Who will provide additional support? E.g. Day care drop off/ pick up.

_____

_____

_____

Who do I need to speak with for approvals (to work flexibly) at work?

_____

_____

_____

What are my career goals for the future? (short and long term)

_____

_____

_____

It can only benefit both yourself and your employer to be talking about these things. Focus on how you can both have your needs met.

If your employer is not flexible or willing to consider being flexible, maybe it's time for a change.

Remember. You are in control of your life. There are always other options.

MUMOLOGY

15 THE MUMMA MENTAL LOAD

Before we go to section 2 on #WarriorWomen Careers and work life, there's something else to talk about that mummas live with on a daily basis. It's called the 'mental load'!

WHAT IS THE MUMMA MENTAL LOAD?

You may have already heard of the term 'mental load' as it's applied to women and mothers. I tend to think it's one of those things that makes us more 'warrior' than we should be.

Think of those times you are in the car, trying to focus on the road. Kids in the back seat wanting food, baby crying. You've just picked them up from school or childcare. You now have to think about getting dinner because the partner doesn't get home until an hour after you. You had a massive Board meeting that day and have 5 billion things to do before the end of the week. The grocery shopping hasn't been done. You need to fit homework in between dinner and bath time. You also need to call your dentist because it's time for the annual check-up.

Sooooooo much to think about and get done! This is the mental load. Organizing the business of family and life stuff that needs to be done on a daily, weekly, monthly and yearly basis. All the planning work somehow seems to fall on the women of the family! And for most of us, it's not always fun!

Australian Census data from 2016 shows that women are still doing the bulk of the housework, between 5 and 14 hours per week, whereas men are doing less than 5 hours of unpaid work in the home per week. Say Whaaaaaaaat? I know, it's 2018. Why is this still happening? This doesn't even consider the mental load, the things we have to 'think' about before any physical unpaid labour even happens.

YOU ASK WHY?

The obvious reason, that we all know, is that we have been socialised this way. Women have been doing this work for centuries. I for one didn't experience a 'different' way of life. My mum stayed home and did all the domestic work while my dad went to work and came home to dinner on the table at 5:30pm every night!

We also seem to still feel the same pressures, regardless of whether we work in paid employment or not, to have a sparkling clean house and be seen to be the "good" mother who doesn't allow their child to eat sugar or processed foods. Maybe even one that makes all their snack foods from scratch (no that's not me).

In some instances, expectations on mothers to be 'better' mothers have exploded into gigantic unrealistic proportions and we have even less time to perform our 'good mother duties' than the mothers before us, because we also have jobs.

This means that while the world is talking about 'work-life balance' we are not only struggling to understand how that can happen (more mental load), but we are trying to 'balance' every member of our family's life while we try to fit work and our own life into that picture as well.

For some of us, giving up the reigns and trusting the other half to be responsible for some of the load, is difficult. We can't bear the thought of things falling apart when we have worked so hard to keep things running on a reasonably even keel. But that right there, my friends, is our undoing. We need to change. So that our Warrior children see how family life SHOULD be done, not how it WAS done (in the '50s). The more we take on, the more we contribute to inequality in the home. That is the truth!

CHANGE THE FUTURE OF #WARRIORWOMEN!

So, either change your own situation or, if your children have not yet been born, make sure you don't fall into the mumma mental load trap before they come along. But how do you do this?

Well, there are quite a few things you can do. The time to take action is now. You need to tell your friends to take action too, because we are all in this together. We can't have our sisters carrying more load than the rest of us.

Here are some ideas for how you can shift some or half of the mental load across to your partner and family members:

1. Go on a mini holiday
For your partner to really feel the effects of your mental load and for you to get a break from the load, you need to book in at least a few days away from your family. Take the girls and go on a girls'

trip. You need to ask your partner to write down the things he does, including housework, but also things he has to think about that need getting done during the time you are away. That way, if he writes things down, you have the start of a list you can use to divide up the tasks when you get home and have that conversation.

2. Stop writing three-page instructions when you leave the house for any amount of time

This of course relates to your mini-break. DO NOT under any circumstances leave a list of things he needs to know. Tell him things he might need to be reminded of such as sports or kids parties, but don't leave any list about anything you would do, especially bedtime routines, food to cook (do not under any circumstances leave pre-cooked meals either) or where to find things. This is your partner's time to fend for himself and really think about his parenting role. Fathers are not babysitters – they are parents!

3. Stop stepping in to avoid disasters (unless it's a safety issue)

If you have issues with control, this one might be difficult for you, but it's essential to the other person's learning and growth. Let them handle the spilled milk or the poo explosion. Let them deal with the tantrum if it's happening in his space and you are in another room. Let him cook the food the way he wants to, especially if it means he may fail at meeting the children's million mealtime demands.

4. Let GO

The house does not have to look like a Vogue Living magazine cover every single day. Nor do your children have to look like models every day. A bit of dust and dirt won't kill anyone (unless you have a family member who is extremely allergic). Ease up on the expectations. Learn to relax in the quieter moments. I know that's easier said than done, but it's important if you want to show your family you can let go of the little things. This is really important for kids to learn also. If they see their mumma having a mental breakdown because there are crumbs on the floor for more than half a day, they will learn that behaviour from you. They'll take it into adulthood.

Part of letting go is also delegating. Once you have that list of all the things you think about and do for your family, you need to assign each task to a person in your family, including yourself and your partner, making sure things are equal and doable.

5. Share the planning

If you are going on a holiday or camping trip, or even on a picnic down the road, everyone should help to plan the event. Kids can pack things, Dads and partners can pack things. If you all get together and plan what you need, then write a list, the burden of remembering everything should not just fall on mumma's shoulders.

WHAT IF WE DON'T SHARE THE LOAD?

Well I think this is a no brainer. If we don't start sharing the mental load, the planning and the tasks – families will be forever reliant on mumma!

Who wants that? Not I said the #WarriorWoman

I for one feel resentment creeping in when I'm the one doing all the thinking and planning and work for the family. Resentment is not healthy for any family.

Crankiness is also another unfortunate by-product of having to do it all. No one likes a cranky mumma.

I also think that the biggest and most important reasons for sharing the load is because we #WarriorWomen want equality in all areas of our lives, not just work. If we start doing it now, our children will follow in our footsteps.

Our sons will continue to expect in their families that the washing will be done, the appointments organized, the social events organized, the holidays planned, the passports arranged... and our daughters will continue to do it all for them. Is that what you want for your daughters? Is this the kind of men we want our boys to grow into? If we want to create a better world for our children. It starts with us now.

SECTION 2

CAREER #WARRIORWOMEN

2 CAREER #WARRIORWOMEN

16 CHANGING CAREERS

> " *Your purpose in life is to find your purpose and give your whole heart and soul to it."*
>
> BUDDHA

Let's face it, we spend most of our adult lives in some form of paid work. Whatever it is, whatever you choose, it should make you want to jump out of bed in the morning.

At any point in our lives, #WarriorWomen may experience uncertainty and dissatisfaction with our work, which usually manifests in that feeling of dread when you're getting ready for work, wondering what kind of crap's coming your way today. This may lead to thinking about a career change or, at least, other options.

Other major life transitions, such as having children, mid-life, redundancy or divorce, can also stir up ideas about needing or wanting to change careers. Sometimes it might just be boredom, the feeling that you are not fulfilling your purpose in this world.

Most of us will change our careers at least once in our lifetime (generation Y and millennials look likely to change careers at least twice in their lifetime and have many more jobs). Whether this be by choice or because of the rapid rate that industries are changing or becoming obsolete, it's now the reality that women (and men) face.

My own daydreams about career change came after having my first child. I couldn't bear the idea of working nine to five, an hour's drive from home, and spending ten hours a day away from my baby in a job that just didn't stir my passions anymore.

I have to admit, a coach at this time would've saved me a whole lot of time and money, because I did try to change my career. I didn't quite get it right.

LOOK BEFORE YOU LEAP

There's a lot to be said for careful consideration of your options when changing careers.

Before children, I was quite fit. I trained five to six times per week. So I thought a great option for me would be to become a personal trainer.

I set out on this new career path thinking I was going to make loads of money and work the hours I wanted to and change people's lives by making them fit and strong. I spent a few thousand dollars on studies to get my personal trainer qualifications. I set up a business name, got myself an Australian Business Number (ABN) and off I went.

Sadly, it turned out I didn't actually enjoy training people who weren't as motivated as me. As much as I loved training myself, I didn't enjoy training other people who didn't REALLY want to work that hard. It was surprising and unexpected, and I really didn't know what to do about it.

I thought, 'How can I make people want to train hard?' I asked other trainers who'd been my mentors and friends how they coped with people who didn't really want to train hard. They said it was all part of the business. There was no solution. They just put up with them and accepted they couldn't help everyone to make the changes in their lives unless they were committed to doing it themselves!

I kept at the personal training for a little while as a supplementary income to my now part-time job. I even trained my colleagues at lunchtime (it was boxing training so I called it Lunch Box. Cute right?). But after I had my first baby, I didn't want to do it anymore. I was probably too sleep deprived.

That was the end of that career.

TAKE TWO

The second attempt I made at changing careers was when I was planning my son's first birthday. I entered a whole new world of crazy at this time in my life (maybe you did too with your first child?). I wanted it jungle themed to honour his South African heritage, and once I started to google, there was no stopping me.

I've since found out this is a first time mum 'thing' that many of us new mums encounter.

Themed plates, balloons, straws, matching 'thank you' tags and party bags (which are called loot bags, apparently!). I thought (and I know I'm not the first new mum to think this), 'WOW! There's so much involved in planning a kids party, I should start up a business for mums who are too busy to plan it themselves.'

I didn't think this through properly. I thought I was going to make tons of money in the kids' party industry and it was going to allow me to have more flexibility in my life. I was wrong.

I did my first gig when one of my beautiful friends employed me to do her daughter's birthday party. I set up a lolly buffet, made cupcakes, labelled everything, set up a photo booth with hand-made props, planned games and really ensured my attention to all the little details.

It looked absolutely stunning, if I do say so myself. However, once the 25 eight-year-old girls were all in the house, screaming at the top of their lungs, for no apparent reason, I came to my second realisation that not only did large groups of screaming children hurt my ears, but I was no children's party entertainer. I had chosen the wrong career, again.

I also realised I was not going to make my fortune (or even minimum wage) doing kids' parties. After spending probably twenty hours planning, preparing and setting up the party for a mere $300, after product costs, I think I came away in deficit. Hardly an entrepreneurial win.

The party was close to a disaster. My friend was gracious. I was distraught. I'd spent a lot of money setting up this party business and now I couldn't bear the thought of having to do this every weekend.

Luckily for me, all was not lost. I found a happy medium. I went into party 'styling'. This meant I could set up lolly buffets, decorate the party and leave before it started. It still meant a lot of work buying, making and preparing the décor, but I didn't have to entertain very excitable children. So, for me, this was the perfect evolution of my business model.

I did lolly buffets/party styling for a number of years and still do it as a hobby on the side. It was never going to make me rich, but it was wonderful to find I had a creative side and to nurture that for the first time in my life.

THIRD TIME LUCKY...

Finally, before my second child was conceived, I looked into coaching with a wonderful friend of mine who was also looking into it. We both got very excited about the possibilities. Now that I am immersed in this field, I know that it is absolutely what I was meant to do with my life.

It is a good fit for me because this work aligns with my core values and beliefs, which is one of the single most important aspects of choosing a new career. Align it with your core beliefs and values. Along with your strengths, skills and abilities.

I learned making loads of money should not be your first priority. If that is your sole motivator for changing careers then you will more than likely fail.

I believe I was put on this earth to help others. Especially my sisters, the #WarriorWomen of the world. My strengths, skills and abilities lie in helping. Coaching for me has opened up my world in terms of how I can help people. Yes, making money is still something I want and value (as it should be for all #WarriorWomen), but it's not my only value. Something that wasn't aligned with all my core values was never going to work.

Your values are what you consider important in life. Becoming aware of your values helps you to assess whether the direction of your life is in line with what is important to you. The following exercise will help you to increase your awareness of your values and the extent to which you are living in line with those values.

This exercise is divided into the four areas of life that are important to us all. Think about each area. Describe your personal values. How do you want to live your life in this area? Be sure to focus on your values rather than your actions/goals.

What is important to me in...

1. Work/education

_____

_____

2. Relationships

_____

_____

3. Leisure

_____

_____

4. Personal growth/health

_____

_____

This exercise should have you thinking about what is important in your life, what is missing. You need to think about what is preventing you from living your life according to your values.

Write down the obstacles getting in your way. Describe those obstacles here (these can range from thoughts and feelings to actual obstacles like money, time, people even):

_____

_____

_____

_____

_____

Finally you need to think about what you can do to take you one step closer to living your values. What actions can you take in each area of your life?

1. Work/education

_____

_____

_____

2. Relationships

_____

_____

_____

3. Leisure

_____

_____

_____

4. Personal growth/health

_____

_____

_____

You now have a list of actions that align you to your values. If you are thinking of a career change, take the steps from the work/education section as your first priority.

2 CAREER #WARRIORWOMEN

17 CAREER CHALLENGES

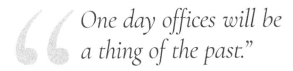

One day offices will be a thing of the past."

SIR RICHARD BRANSON

My quest to help other women achieve their hopes and dreams has shown me the real barriers women, in particular mothers, face in being able to pursue their career aspirations. These are barriers that you too may have experienced.

WORK-LIFE BALANCE WHAT?

I think in many areas of work life, society is taking a while to catch up with the new world order. Many employers are making changes to their employee conditions, but there are many industries still making it hard for women to pursue careers and achieve a work-life balance. That is the flexibility that many of us want once we have children. In fact, even without having had children, we all want and need flexibility in our working lives don't we?

What I hate most is the sense I get from people (both women and men) that you have to choose. It's either the job first or the children first. According to this theory, stay-at-home mums choose not to have a career because they want to raise their children full time. On the other side of the coin, full-time working mums put their careers first.

This is a load of rubbish, as all you #WarriorWomen know too well.

We women have to make difficult decisions every day about our priorities. Is it the school assembly, the work conference or Board meeting; if our child is sick, do we stay at home or get someone to take care of them while we go to work for that meeting we can't miss?

The struggle is real. A lot of it is unnecessary if only we could be more flexible in our work.

TRUE BALANCE

What we need is real life flexibility. So when we come to make decisions about career and family, we 'feel' like we have options and we 'feel' like our choices are supported by our employers. I'll talk more about this important point later.

When I was getting legal advice for writing this book, the solicitor told me this is what women in the legal profession need – that is, transition coaching through maternity. They struggle to have the flexibility and balance when they have children. I thought about that. I realised there's a lot of work to be done, particularly in traditionally male-dominated, patriarchal professions like the legal field (sorry, guys, I'm sure not *all* legal firms are patriarchal).

I'm not saying every woman wants to work part-time – or full-time for that matter – after having children, but I believe every woman (and man) wants at least the flexibility to be there for their children when it matters most to them. As well as a career that satisfies them. Some of the things I think help to create flexibility is flexible working hours, start and finish times, working from home, working at night or on weekends as a start.

THE 'MOTHERHOOD PENALTY'

Some women who have high-pressure, long-hour, corporate or executive jobs find that after having children, they can't or don't want to sustain that kind of life, and so, they need to change careers or take a backward step.

This might be a positive change or a reluctant one for them, because most of the corporate world hasn't yet caught on to flexible working arrangements and still believe that if you're not working a 12-hour office day , then you're not working hard enough.

Surprisingly, in my experience, these attitudes come from both women and men, which is a big part of the problem! If women and men can't come together on this issue and agree that flexibility is the way forward, then it's my opinion that we just won't evolve in the workforce. Equality for women in work places will never happen like that.

Working #WarriorWomen suffer this thing called the 'motherhood penalty' (yes, it's a thing). The 'motherhood penalty' is a term coined by sociologists to describe the fact that because women take time out from work to have children, they often come back to a job part time and are either given low-responsibility (aka mind-numbing) projects or they must take a step backwards because they can't – according to their employers –fulfil the duties of the role they once held.

The 'motherhood penalty' means mothers earn less money, are less likely to be interviewed and hired, or promoted, are more likely to work part time or in jobs that are below their skill and education levels, and are more likely to be considered less capable and committed.

THE PART-TIME PENALTY

As we know, that's all bollocks. There are plenty of industries that won't promote women in part-time roles or even offer them their positions part time after returning to work from having children. You may have experienced this yourself.

My own experience of the 'motherhood penalty' has plagued my career. Returning to work after my first child, my manager at the time (whom I had a great deal of respect for and who happened to be a woman) told me I'd never get a higher grade job working part time.

That was a blow for me, because I knew I was capable at that higher level and that there were people at that level working part time already. I couldn't understand what the actual problem was with women working part time.

Was it women from the 'old school', who had to either work full time or give up their aspirations to work in higher grade jobs after children, who didn't want to see the change for other women because they'd missed out? Was it a belief that women working part time didn't get the same amount of work done? (Which can often be resolved through job share.)

I knew for a fact that there were people in my team working full time who didn't get as much work done as I did in the three days I was in the office. So it made me sad to think this draconian view could be perpetuated by other women in my industry.

Over the years, I've had some very supportive managers who wanted me to act in the higher grades and gave me those opportunities, but I have to say, that one conversation made **me** lose my confidence to actually apply for roles at that level, knowing I only wanted a part time position.

THE SAD FACTS

According to Diversity Council Australia, mothers experience a 17% loss in wages over their lifetime. They take a 4% pay cut after the birth of their first child and a 9% pay cut for each subsequent child. Women not only earn 18% less than men but working mothers also earn 22% less than females without children in the workforce.[4]

Most of the time, women who choose to have children are faced with the challenge of how they will balance paid work and motherhood, and this can cause a great deal of stress to women as they make decisions about what area of their life they will need to make sacrifices in.

---

[4]   http://m.dailylife.com.au/news-and-views/news-features/the-hidden-penalties-of-being-a-mother-in-the-workforce by Erin O'Dwyer 05/04/15

Why does it have to be this way? Most women I know with children work harder because they know they have less time to commit to it – this makes them more efficient, not less efficient. It also makes their lives more stressful because they take work home when they should be spending time with their children.

YOU SAY YOU WANT A REVOLUTION?

Well I do too! A flexible workforce is necessary for those mums – all parents, for that matter – doing jobs they love and don't want to leave. But for this to happen, the workforce needs to radically change.

It's time for a #WarriorWomen working revolution. If your employer isn't flexible and isn't open to exploring the possibilities for more flexibility in your role or a similar role, then maybe it's time for you to consider a career or workplace change.

If your really love where you work and want to stay then definitely have the important conversations with your boss about how you can make it work so you both get what you need. Champion flexible work practices and do some research on the benefits of flexible working to back yourself up.

Remember, if people won't listen then you do have the freedom and power to make your own decisions about your life!

There are a number of companies starting up that help professional women find part-time roles doing what they're qualified and experienced to do. Rather than stepping down the ladder, these organisations make it easier for women to stay at their level in their chosen fields and offer the flexibility professional women and mothers need.

There are employers in small business who may not necessarily have the budget to employ executives/professionals like you at full-time rates but can definitely pay a part-time wage and, therefore, get the professional services they want.

Join this revolution, get out of the job that makes you sick with worry and stress, and put your own needs first (you deserve this).

Check out www.beamaustralia.com.au for part-time professional work and start working on your terms in the job you love!

Now might also be a good time to think about your career challenges and aspirations and determine if you need to make some changes. Here are some preliminary questions to ask yourself:

Is my employment flexible enough to meet my current and future needs?

Yes/No

What else do I need in this job to keep me here and is it available to me?

_____

_____

_____

Who do I need to talk to to ensure my needs are met? (employer, mentor, coach)

_____

_____

What other options do I have? This is a possibility question that requires you to think outside the box and come up with alternatives to your current situation that would be acceptable for you in your career/work life.

_____

_____

_____

This exercise may have got you thinking about doing something different – the next chapter will help you work out how to go about that!

2 CAREER #WARRIORWOMEN

18 COACHING CAREER CHANGE

" *Follow your bliss and the universe will open doors where there were only walls."*

JOSEPH CAMPBELL

Maybe you changed your whole perspective on life after having children? Maybe your children are grown now and life is different for you, you now have time to focus more on yourself?

Maybe you've travelled a lot lately and it has opened your eyes to all the possibilities for learning and life experience and you want more?

Whatever is going on for you now, career change is possible.

I know my perspective on work and life changed when I had my first child. I absolutely wanted to be more fulfilled in the work I did and do something with purpose. I needed the time away from my baby to be meaningful.

If you don't know what you love anymore because your life has changed, a coach or mentor might be the best first step for you.

There are many tips and strategies you can follow to ensure you are also aligned with your core values and beliefs like those we have done in the earlier chapters (if you haven't done those activities I encourage you to give it a go). You need to make sure you are driven by what you believe and value in life, by what you are passionate about.

It's a big thing to make the decision to change careers. You might be feeling scared, uncertain, anxious, excited. If it's your choice to change careers, congratulations. What an exciting time for you – the possibilities are endless. Explore each and every one of them.

As women, we often think we don't have the skills needed. We spend a lot of time thinking about changing career but not enough time invested in actually taking action and 'doing it'.

All you need is a whole lot of belief in yourself and a PLAN. Remember, coaching is all about setting goals and then actioning the plan to get the results you aim for.

One #WarriorWoman I spoke to, Sarah, made the career change from public servant to private practitioner and found it one of the best decisions of her life;

'In making this transition, my overall feelings were excitement, joy and relief to be "my own boss". I was surprised by how easy it was for me to walk away from my government position where I'd worked for the past eight years.'

She found the transition extremely positive and realised (what most women realise once they make the decision to change career or go out on their own);

'That I am even more determined than I thought -

That I have skills that people want (shouldn't be surprising, I know, but I do have the tendency to underestimate my abilities)'.

WHEN WILL YOU KNOW IT'S TIME TO CHANGE CAREER?

Speaking from experience there are usually some pretty obvious signs that we choose to ignore most of the time or put in the 'too hard basket'.

If you're not sure if you should look at a change in career, here are some of the signs you may be ignoring:

- You feel as though your skills and abilities could be used better elsewhere doing something more meaningful or purposeful (this was me).
- You're tired and exhausted all the time.
- You get depressed about going to work every day (and it's not about leaving your children).
- You can't relate to the work, you hate it and couldn't care less about it!

- Your salary doesn't matter to you anymore and doesn't make up for how much you don't enjoy your work.

If you experience any – or all – of these feelings on a regular basis, then I'm guessing you probably need to re-evaluate your career plans. If you really hate your job, it's time, right?

You might be feeling **stuck**, wanting to change but not wanting to risk the job security you have. This is a pretty common feeling and one you can combat by taking things slowly.

Nobody says you have to change your career in a week, month or year. It may take a few years, especially if you want to study something new or start up a business. So, take it one step at a time."

It's also good to remember you have more than one chance at changing career. If the first option doesn't work out, then you go down another path (like for me I tried two new careers before I found my true purpose). You can also tweak your business model or pathway along the way.

STRATEGIES FOR CAREER PLANNING

Here are some pointers for getting your new career off the ground.

- BELIEVE it can happen – once we believe it, others will too!

- Network like crazy – try and meet new people who may be in the industry you're thinking about. Hang out with lots of different types of people. EXPAND your world and connections. Don't necessarily start with job search and recruitment agencies – some of the best jobs you can find are through people you meet and the relationships you build.

- Stop analysing and take action – if you're all up in your own head with so many unanswered questions, go out and get them answered. Volunteer, shadow someone at work, get some work experience or try a job part time - think outside the box.

- An NLP strategy that can help propel you towards your ultimate career is modelling (not catwalk modelling, although that may be appropriate if you think so). I mean the behaviour kind of modelling. This is a key premise of NLP, in which you model your behaviour on the successful behaviours of others. Find people who are doing what you'd love to do and have had great success in their field. Read about their journey, find out what they did and didn't do to get there and start doing these things yourself.

COACHING QUESTIONS FOR CAREER PLANNING

Here are some questions you can ask yourself now to get yourself started – write them down and make sure you keep in mind your core values and beliefs;

Think back to a time when you achieved something you are really proud of – what was it?

_____

_____

_____

What strengths and abilities did you use? (Ultimately, knowing your strengths can help you to market yourself with confidence and target the right role.)

_____

_____

_____

Now think of your present job, what do you need to leave behind in order to move forward?

_____

_____

_____

What aspects of your work are important and fulfilling that you can focus on now?

_____

_____

What do you want more of in your work life? What are your future job goals?

_____

_____

What are the possibilities for a changed role within your current organisation (if that's an option)?

_____

_____

What are your financial and social needs?

_____

_____

_____

What have you been afraid to do?

_____

_____

_____

What initial step can you take right now to move you in the right direction?

_____

_____

_____

YOUR STRENGTHS

I'm a massive advocate for focusing on people's strengths rather than their weaknesses, especially in the workplace.

Key strategies to focus on are; making sure you not only know your strengths, but that you're also passionate about those things.

Ask other people what they think your strengths are and see how you feel about what they say.

Other people can see your strengths when you may not be able to. So listen to them, but also listen to your heart or gut (whichever organ speaks to you) and move towards your passions.

YOUR PASSIONS

Passion is key to finding happiness in work. If you don't know what you're passionate about, then try to think of things you like to do with your spare time.

Be real, be realistic and get a coach to help you find those core values, beliefs and things that will make your heart sing every day you get up to go and do the work you love. You can even call me!

The key mantra to keep in the forefront of your mind when embarking on your career change is:

"What you believe, you can achieve."

So, get out there and start taking some action!

To expand on the previous activity in this chapter this next activity aims to get you thinking about your strengths and passions in more detail.

1. What did I want to be when I was a child and why?

_____

_____

_____

2. What am I passionate about?

_____

_____

_____

3. What do I love doing with my spare time?

_____

_____

4. What are my strengths in life and on the job? (Create two lists here.)

Life	Work

5. What do other people say I am good at? (If your significant others have never told you then you need to ask them.)

_____

_____

_____

6. What new skills have I found in myself since having children that might be applicable in the workplace?

_____

_____

_____

7. What would I do if there were no barriers (like money, time etc) and I could be anything I wanted to be?

_____

_____

_____

Once you write down the answers to these questions, you may see a pattern. You may see something you've never thought of before and wonder where on earth that came from!

That happened to me the first time I did this exercise. It turns out I've always wanted to be a travel writer and get paid to travel the world and write about my experiences. That was unexpected. Though, I might have to wait a few years before I get to that one!

Once you've considered your responses above, start thinking about what you could do with your strengths and the things other people say you're good at. It just might be the way to your bliss, your purpose for being here! Deep but absolute truth!

Note: Once you start thinking about possibilities, your brain, that has been very well conditioned to find ALL the reasons why things are NOT possible will start throwing you arguments, buts and questions like, "How will you do that Einstein?"

You need to be very aware of your thoughts at this point. Try to park the doubts and negative thoughts that come into your mind or just respond to yourself with "that's interesting' and stay on your positive mind path.

Something might come up that you've always wanted to do but have never explored before because of barriers (real or not). So the next step is to spend some time here thinking about the 'how'. I want you to spend a bit of time on this and focus on ALL the options.

1. What resources do I need to get myself into a job/career/ business like that? Go crazy, think outside the box, you need at least 10 ideas here.

_____

_____

_____

_____

_____

2. Who do I need to speak to? (People in the industry, education providers, Facebook groups, people already doing the job/career etc.)

_____

_____

_____

_____

3. What are all the things I can do right now that would take me one step closer to that job? (Go wild, no limitations)

_____

_____

_____

In asking yourself these questions, you're opening up a new reality for yourself. Everything's possible. As you consider all your possibilities, you allow your brain to set down new pathways, which if you continue to think like this, will lead you to the results you're after.

In the coaching world, we call this 'possibility thinking.' As the saying goes, you're only limited by your imagination. Believing in yourself, your strengths and your abilities is key to catapulting yourself forward in your life.

Alice: This is impossible
The Mad Hatter: Only
if you believe it is

ALICE IN WONDERLAND

Now, these final questions are to get you taking action on your journey to find the job, career, business you were meant for.

1. What is the first step you will take to move you towards your new career?

_____

2. When will you do it? (Be exact with date and time if necessary.)

_____

_____

3. Who will you tell you are doing it ? (for accountability)

_____

_____

Time to get going on those action steps. Make a daily, weekly and monthly plan for how you will keep moving towards the realisation of your new goals.

SECTION 3

MID LIFE

3 MID LIFE

19 MID-LIFE CRISIS

" *People may call what happens at midlife 'a crisis,' but it's not. It's an unraveling - a time when you feel a desperate pull to live the life you want to live, not the one you're 'supposed' to live."*

BRENE BROWN

So the mid-life crisis is actually a thing for women, too! Who'd have thought! Never in my life did I think it was something us #WarriorWomen would even need to go through. It turns out this is one major life transition we can and do go through!

Don't despair, though, it's not a 'crisis' for everyone. In fact, modern research suggests it's not a 'crisis' at all but a re-evaluation[5].

It can also happen at the same time as other life transitions, like divorce/separation, and can prompt a career transition, too!

We don't all feel the need to go out and buy flashy sports cars, but it can actually be a time of empowerment and taking back the reigns of our lives.

YOUR TRUE SELF

Like all our life transitions, mid-life can be an opportunity for positive growth and personal development. It's a time when we may feel like the chains of responsibility are loosening (if your children are getting older and more independent) and we may feel less constrained by social rules around our identity and style.

Psychologist Carl Jung suggested that mid-life is a time when we can abandon the socially constructed ideas of who we are and start to become our 'truer selves'.

If you've spent most of your life being the person you think you should be rather than the person you truly are you might get to mid-life and want to become more like your truer self. This might create a little crisis (or a big one, depending on your personality type and whether you tend to go a bit cray-cray like me).

---

[5]   Fielder and Panchal in Palmer and Panchal, Developmental Coaching, Life Transitions and Generational Perspectives

YOUR UNIQUE CRISIS

Women and men go through mid-life transitions differently. We women tend to become less concerned with relationships, while men become more focused on relationships. This can mean tricky times in hetero-marriages and may also lead to relationship breakdowns, causing even further life transitions.

The thing that's strange is that women's mid-life crises get very little attention in popular culture. I mentioned the flashy cars before, but that is a man's mid-life crisis. Very rarely, if ever, do you see a woman depicted in a hot red sports car chasing hot young men around town.

#WarriorWomen are more likely to feel a bit wobbly at mid-life because of family problems or feeling as though we haven't lived up to our own expectations or goals. At mid-life women might be feeling as though we've pushed our needs to the side to meet the needs of others for way too long.

At this stage in life women, can feel invisible. It doesn't help that in the media and movies middle aged women are not generally celebrated.

On the other hand, men are more likely to be worried about work or career issues.

Women's mid-life transition or crises (I'll use these terms inter-changeably just so you know I mean either thing at any given time) are characterised by feelings of depression, emptiness, change in desires, bewilderment and wonder at where on earth all of these feelings have suddenly come from![6]

MY MID-LIFE CRAZY

My mid-life crisis came from left of field. To be honest, I didn't know I was having one at the time.

Something happened to me a few years ago that was a bit of a mental breakdown. Looking back, I realise it was driven by a mid-life crisis of epic proportions and a turning point that would change my life forever in ways I had not even imagined.

I'd just turned 40. Some say this is the start of mid-life; I didn't subscribe to that view, but I was restless. I was over my life, I was bored and I didn't have any direction. I'd spent the last four years working part-time in what I thought was my career job, but it was sapping the life out of me. I felt like I wasn't being an effective member of society – I wasn't being an effective member of anything!

My life at home was becoming mundane. I wasn't getting any joy out of the things I used to, like training and running and boxing. I woke up most days miserable and wondering 'is this really it?'

And my husband and I had stopped putting an effort into our relationship. So much so that it came to a breaking point. Things got quite bad. Everything in my life turned upside down, and we both had to search our souls to find our way back to each other again.

---

[6]   Selinger Morris, 2013, "The female midlife crisis."

This was only the beginning of my mid-life crisis/transition.

I decided I wanted to change my career.

My husband decided he wanted to have another child! This was momentous because we didn't manage the life transition after our first child too well, so we'd previously agreed he'd remain an only child.

And so with a few deep and meaningful conversations and coming up with ideas on how we could make it all happen, we agreed on doing both!

So my mid-life transition turned out to be the best and worst year of my life – some of my darkest moments and some of my best.

When we came out of the hazy fog that was relationship counselling and coaching, we went on the best family holiday ever. Just after my 41st birthday I was up the duff for a second time and really excited to be adding to our little family.

I'd also started my coaching course and realised I'd found the 'thing' I was meant to be doing with my life. It was the mid-life crisis I had to have to find my true self!

3 MID LIFE

20 THE MID-LIFE TRANSITION

> " *Midlife: When the Universe grabs your shoulders and tells you "I'm not f-king around, use the gifts you were given."*

BRENE BROWN

Mid-life is the time we ask the BIG questions (I asked these questions of myself in my teens but, of course, had very few useful or insightful answers to give myself at the time – what teenager does?).

At this stage of our lives, many of us ask:

- *Who am I?*
- *What am I doing with my life?*
- *Why am I here and*
- *What is my life purpose?*

We're approaching the middle of our lives. We're about to embark on the second half. We're in a kind of 'make or break' half time where we have to make some decisions about what we want the second half to bring.

This stirs up a whole host of questions about our identity and what we want to do with this second half of our lives.

Some say we face our mortality and start to think about our legacy (I can't say I've thought of those things on a conscious level, but my behaviours may just well indicate otherwise).

I like to think of it as us deciding how we want to make our mark on the world so our one life wasn't wasted on cooking, cleaning and playing house (not that there's anything wrong with that if that's your joy in life).

Some of the things that come up in mid-life revolve around other life transitions. I mentioned earlier that marriages often break down in mid-life, bringing with it the major life transition of divorce. This can happen because some women may have been in unhappy marriages, their children have grown and they no longer feel the pressure or expectation to stay married. They may also feel the effects of the 'empty nest', with children getting older and not being home as much.

It's probably not as much an issue for parents from generations X and Y, because women of those generations are more likely to have worked while bringing up children. Some women who chose to be stay-at-home parents for all those years now find themselves lost without children to chase after, cook and wash for and organise. This can put a strain on the relationship, as sometimes couples realise they have little in common without the children to focus on.

Careers may also change around mid-life, bringing with it a career life transition. We may think about what we have done in our career, where we are going and that if we are not on track to change the world, then it's time to change direction.

For many women, their careers relate closely to their sense of identity, so if we are having an existential identity crisis, this may mean a complete change in career.

SECTION 3 MID LIFE

STRATEGIES FOR MID-LIFE

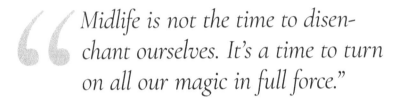

Midlife is not the time to disenchant ourselves. It's a time to turn on all our magic in full force."

MARIANNE WILLIAMSON

Because mid life can represent a major turning point in a woman's life, there are things you can do to make it a more purposeful, healthy and positive transition.

Below are some things you might find useful to help you navigate the mid-life transition.

STEP 1 – DO SOMETHING HEALTHY

Health and well-being have always been important. Now more than ever it is time to start taking better care of your physical and mental health.

I started yoga this year, after never in my life thinking I would want to do yoga. I'd tried it in my late 20s and I actually fell asleep in the class only to be woken by my friend who'd dragged me there. Now, though, I have to say it surprised me how much I love it. I can't do a lot of the poses yet. I find myself falling over a lot, but by the end of the class I lay there in peace and feel calm and rested. This is something very new to me. Something I know my body and mind both need.

I was never a person who was happy unless I was going 'hell for leather' in terms of exercise. So yoga and meditation was always something 'other people' did.

Now I'm hooked. I love the feeling of stretching out all my tired muscles and my tired mind. Don't get me wrong, I still love a good boxing session and I have to run, even though my body yells at me afterwards, but I think it's that thing called 'balance' everyone is talking about and I'd never gotten around to trying.

So I'm going to coach you to do the same thing. Try something new. Eat new foods. Think of this next phase of life as a new adventure. You need to get healthy for it. You need to be balanced!

STEP 2 – REVIEW YOUR BELIEFS ABOUT YOURSELF AND YOUR AGE

If you've placed limitations on yourself because of your age, I strongly encourage you to revisit these.

Age is just a number. Whatever you believe about age can be changed. If you say negative things about yourself that relate back to your age I want you to become aware of it. I want you to remind yourself that beliefs are things you've been told by others.

They're not necessarily based on fact. If you have a negative belief about your age, like something you can't or shouldn't do because 'you're too old for that', I bet you wouldn't be able to find reputable evidence to support that belief. The only thing stopping you from doing it is you!

Now is the time to write down all the things you wanted to do but haven't yet done in your life. Start making plans for how you can go about making them happen. Tell the Debbie Downer in your head to 'go away' and start believing you can do whatever you set out to achieve, all you have to do is believe (rhyming unintended!)

STEP 3 – REDISCOVER YOUR LOVE

Not for *who* but *what*! What is it that makes your heart sing, that sets your soul on fire? What is it that used to do that?

It could be painting, singing or pole dancing or writing. It could be absolutely anything. What inspires you or brought you joy when you were younger?

It's time to reconnect with yourself and with the things that you are passionate about. Spend time on this. Think back to the times you were doing things that made you happy. Write them down and then begin to put in place plans for doing these things. If you don't know or you already do the things that bring you joy, then try something new. See where it leads. The possibilities are endless.

STEP 4 – PRACTICE GRATITUDE

This is one for every stage of life, through every transition, in good times and bad. Practicing gratitude reminds you of all the things you have in life, instead of all the things you don't have, and it reminds you of all the possibilities life has to offer.

An exercise to help you to connect with the positive things in your life and build on your strengths is to start a gratitude journal. I mentioned this before and think it's a useful strategy for every person, regardless of being in a life transition or not.

The way this process usually works is: you write about the people and 'things' you have and do, then when you exhaust those and really open up your mind to being grateful you will find the little things, like the five minutes peace you got or the fact someone left you some toilet paper on the roll first thing in the morning!

When you practice gratitude, you find there are so many things in your life to be grateful for and you begin to see the good in your life far more than the bad. This in turn brings more good things into your life.

Practicing gratitude is an NLP technique that helps you to re-train your brain, a term I'm sure you have heard before. It's about focussing on the positive, keeping your thoughts and feelings positive (as a priority), which in turn has your brain following positive neural pathways which sees you seeking out the positive far more than the negative.

STEP 5 – DO SOMETHING FOR OTHERS

What difference could you make in your community? How can you make other people's lives better? Being altruistic is good for our health and makes us feel good, quite literally. Being kind and generous releases oxytocin, a hormone that helps us to bond and make stronger connections.

Maybe you have a neighbour who has just had a baby and might be lonely or tired or both. You could help them by watching/cuddling the baby while they go for a walk, or sit with them and make them a cup of tea that they actually get to drink hot (Yes this was on my wish list after both my babies).

You could volunteer for a local charity or at a school. You could go and talk to people in aged care homes (and learn a thing or two from the wise sages housed in these heart breaking places).

Maybe you are really good at something and could teach others at a local community centre – like knitting, crocheting, art, dancing! Whatever it is you can do, everyone has something to give back.

There are so many things you can do that gives back to your community. The possibilities are endless.

STEP 6 – PUT YOURSELF FIRST FOR ONCE

This one is a hard one for women who have always put their families before everything for most of their adult life.

I'm here to say that 'yes' it might be hard but you need to start doing it before you become bitter and sad about all the things you didn't do for yourself when you get to the end of your life.

Start by doing one thing per day that is for you and you alone.

Start thinking about the things you want, the things you deserve and how you can go about bringing them into your life.

You deserve to live the fullest life possible and now is the time to make that happen. Write it down in your journal at the end of the day to make yourself accountable to yourself.

The following blank pages are for your own thoughts and ideas, goals and plans for action. Be bold in your commitment to yourself and your dreams.

_____

_____

_____

_____

_____

_____

_____

_____

_____

_____

_____

_____

A FINAL NOTE TO ALL THE AMAZING #WARRIORWOMEN

All the strategies and tools I have shared in this book for some of the life transitions we #WarriorWomen go through form part of my coaching practice and come from a range of coaching resources. There are no boundaries around them. There are no boundaries for you in choosing to live your best life whilst also living the life of a parent, employee or business owner, wife, partner and friend.

As women we have so many opportunities to stand beside other women and raise them up, uplifting not only their hearts and minds but our own at the same time.

Choose your tribe or tribes carefully. Ultimately the women you have by your side will contribute to the success of your life. You want the very best right there beside you so they can bring out the very best in you.

Every transition we women experience is an opportunity to re-evaluate our tribe and live our best life.

Choose your life with passion, intention and commitment. Choose to move forward not backwards, lean in to new experiences and lean on the #WarriorWomen who can help you achieve your dreams.

I want to thank the tribe of #WarriorWomen I have in my life. You fill my cup, you bring me endless amounts of joy and love and you remind me of how lucky I am every single day.

My hope is that all women will have at least one tribe behind them, supporting them and loving them for who they are. Without them, we are less!

With love, laughter and light in my heart I thank you for being a part of this journey with me and I wish you all the very best for your journey.

Feel free to connect with me on Facebook, Instagram or email Fiona@minddesigncoach.com

Fiona xo

APPENDIX

SO, WHAT IS THIS NLP (NEURO LINGUISTIC PROGRAMMING)?

When I first started studying NLP, I could barely contain my excitement - I knew I'd found the tools I needed to take my coaching practice and life to the next level.

I've always had a love for anything to do with human behaviour and the human mind. In high school, I was one of those kids who people came to with their problems and I really wanted to help them. My early studies started in psychology, sociology and then social work and now coaching and NLP.

NLP was developed by Dr Richard Bandler and John Grinder, an unlikely duo who met in the 1970s and pooled their knowledge of psychology (Bandler) and linguistics (Grinder) after studying the best communicators and leaders of their generation and generations past, to build a model of communication skills. NLP looks at how we structure our experiences, how we think about our values and beliefs, how we build our internal world and give it meaning.[7]

---

[7] O'Connor and Lages Coaching with NLP

Big names in the coaching world, like Tony Robbins and Paul McKenna, were students of NLP and have also built their empires around the premises of NLP.

The thing about NLP is that the techniques are not long drawn out psychological events. We can make changes quickly using simple techniques, some of which I share here in this book to use on yourself.

The premise behind NLP that I love the most and encourage everyone to embrace is that if you truly believe that you can achieve what you want you will find a way to achieve it. There is a feedback loop where what you believe determines how you act, how you act then determines what results you get and the results you get determine your beliefs.

According to Richard Bandler, happy and successful people have a lot of useful beliefs about themselves, the goals they want to achieve and the resources they need to achieve them. They believe they deserve to have what they want and how true is that!

REFERENCES

1. Elizabeth Kubler-Ross, 1969, On Death and Dying

2. http://www.humanrights.gov.au/news/stories/pregnancy-report-reveals-personal-and-financial-cost-discrimination

3. http://m.dailylife.com.au/news-and-views/news-features/the-hidden-penalties-of-being-a-mother-in-the-workforce by Erin O'Dwyer 05/04/15

4. Selinger Morris, 2013, "The female midlife crisis."

5. O'Connor and Lages Coaching with NLP

ABOUT THE AUTHOR

Fiona grew up in southern Sydney, moved to the other side - the Northern beaches - in her early 20s, lived in London for a few years and then found her way back to southern Sydney, where she now lives with her husband and two boys.

Fiona's career has spanned a number of helping professions. With degrees in psychology and social work, she is now immersed in the coaching world with her coaching business, Mind Design Coaching. She is also a children's WISDOM Coach, certified through Adventures in Wisdom™.

She has both national and international clients.

Fiona's passion is helping women and children to take their lives to the next level by changing their minds and supporting them to design the lives they want.